KABBALAH

A Brief Introduction for
CHRISTIANS

Kabbalah:
A Brief Introduction for Christians

2006 First Printing
© 2006 by Tamar Frankiel

Library of Congress Cataloging-in-Publication Data
Frankiel, Tamar, 1946–
Kabbalah : a brief introduction for Christians / Tamar Frankiel.
    p. cm.
Includes bibliographical references.
ISBN-13: 978-1-58023-303-3 (quality pbk.)
ISBN-10: 1-58023-303-1 (quality pbk.)
1. Cabala. 2. Cabala and Christianity. I. Title.
BM525.F7475 2006
296.1'6—dc22

2006023709

10   9   8   7   6   5   4   3   2   1

Manufactured in the United States of America
Cover Design: Jenny Buono

For People of All Faiths, All Backgrounds
Published by Jewish Lights Publishing
A Division of LongHill Partners, Inc.
Sunset Farm Offices, Route 4, P.O. Box 237
Woodstock, VT 05091
Tel: (802) 457-4000   Fax: (802) 457-4004
www.jewishlights.com

Also available in this series

The Jewish Approach to God: A Brief Introduction for Christians
by Rabbi Neil Gillman

Jewish Holidays: A Brief Introduction for Christians
by Rabbi Kerry M. Olitzky and Rabbi Daniel Judson

Jewish Ritual: A Brief Introduction for Christians
by Rabbi Kerry M. Olitzky and Rabbi Daniel Judson

Jewish Spirituality: A Brief Introduction for Christians
by Rabbi Lawrence Kushner

CONTENTS

Acknowledgments

MY OWN PERSONAL DISCOVERY of Kabbalah was not planned in any way. As I look back, I see that strange quality of a spiritual journey—I did not really make decisions about it. I found myself pulled, drawn forward, as if by an ineffable force. Perhaps there is no better example of causation from the future. In a person's life, of course, the future is not yet defined; the actual future depends on one's actions. But the fact that *something* is there, pulling one forward, is not to be doubted. So it was with my journey into Jewish spirituality, which involved descending (as the mystics say) into the intricate world of Kabbalah.

I am very grateful to God for the direction my life has taken. And I also want to thank those whom God provided along the way to bestow gifts and offer the gentle pushes I needed to move forward.

My professors in graduate studies in history of religions at Miami University and the University of Chicago gave me skills in research and critical thinking that have supported me throughout the years, even though many of them would be surprised at the kinds of treasures I chose to mine with those skills. My rabbinic teachers, many from the Hasidic traditions of Chabad-Lubavitch and Breslov, have been the best guides I could imagine through the concepts of Jewish mysticism because they were willing to teach and reteach basics. They are too many to mention, but I must thank Rabbi Chaim Dalfin, who first taught me *Tanya,* a classic of Hasidic philosophy; Rabbi Chaim Citron, who modeled a meaningful approach to textual analysis; and Rabbi Avrohom Czapnik, who inspired me with his way of bringing out practical implications of each mystical insight. I am fortunate also to have been able to work with Rabbi Aaron Parry on other projects; some of what I learned from him has been incorporated here.

I am grateful also for all those who are working so diligently to translate and interpret materials that have been inaccessible for so many decades and centuries. The number of books on Jewish mysticism available in English to the average reader today would simply astound our ancestors. Especially, I want to mention Rabbis Chaim Kramer and Avraham Greenbaum and the Breslov Research Institute, whose work in disseminating Rabbi Nachman's teachings is a model of excellence, combining thoroughness with a passion for spiritual truth. My anchor through all these studies has been the wisdom of Rabbi Abraham Isaac Kook. Paulist Press published an edition of selections of his writings more than twenty-five years ago, which my husband and I received as a wedding present—now the most-thumbed book in our library. A few more selections have become available in English since then, and I have also been fortunate to study pieces of his original Hebrew writings. When more of his work is translated, surely he will be regarded as one of the great visionaries of our time.

Some of the currents of my spiritual life began to flow more surely together about ten years ago. In 1996, I met Connie Kaplan and became an avid student of her teachings about dreams and soul contracts. I became more and more certain that the information she was transmitting supported and enhanced my work in Jewish mysticism. When she began her doctoral work in Creation Spirituality in 1998, she clued me into the exciting work of mathematical cosmologist Brian Swimme and biologist Rupert Sheldrake. A while later, my colleague and friend at Claremont School of Theology, Ann Taves, introduced me to David Griffin, whose work on parapsychology and philosophy fascinated and encouraged me. All these friends were coming to their explorations of spirituality from a variety of Christian backgrounds. I had the opportunity to teach courses on theology and Jewish mysticism at the University of California, Riverside, which helped more pieces of the puzzle come together.

In the meantime, working on two books on prayer with Judy Greenfeld deepened my studies in the practical aspects of mysticism. She, along with Randi Rose, Toba August, and Joyce Kirsch, listened patiently to my early attempts to expound the Kabbalah's teachings about the *sefirot* as I was struggling to understand and integrate them into my life. Other students in seminars I taught with Judy and Connie gave me valuable feedback on my work. I am deeply indebted to all these people.

A few more thanks are due: to my Kabbalah class in the summer of 2000, who helped me fine-tune the presentation—especially to Dena Glaser, Sara Koplin, and Leah Schnall; to Randi, Sara, and Anne Brener, who read early versions of *The Gift of Kabbalah: Discovering the Secrets of Heaven, Renewing Your Life on Earth* (Jewish Lights) on which this book is based; to my students and colleagues at the Academy for Jewish Religion, California, where I have taught mysticism, liturgy, and comparative religion for the past five years; and to Stuart M. Matlins, publisher of Jewish Lights, Emily Wichland, and all the staff at Jewish Lights who helped bring this work into final production.

One caveat: I do not pretend to be an authority on Kabbalah, only an explorer with a few talents to contribute. I can say that I have thought deeply about Jewish mystical teachings and similar teachings in other traditions and have brought to bear the knowledge that is available to me at present, without attempting to make it acceptable to any particular party or denomination. Of course, I take full responsibility for any errors of fact or interpretation.

I hope this book will enable its readers to see God, the universe, and each of us participating in the unfolding of creation. My great desire is that we all can live from a vision of "unbroken wholeness," to use physicist David Bohm's phrase, and of the divine oneness behind apparent multiplicity. In that way, we can perhaps hope to fulfill what the rabbinic tradition identified as the human task: to "make a dwelling place" for God, or, as the Hasidic masters say, to infuse the entire world with godliness.

INTRODUCTION:
A NOTE ON THE
HISTORY OF KABBALAH

KABBALAH, THE POPULAR TERM for Jewish mysticism, comes
from a Hebrew root that means "to receive"; thus, Kabbalah is
the received tradition. The term was originally used to refer
only to medieval Jewish mysticism, but now its usage is much
expanded. Jewish mysticism originated, probably several centuries BCE, in the study of esoteric aspects of the written
Torah (the first five books of the Bible), the contemplation of
prophetic visions like those of Ezekiel and Isaiah, and apoca-
lyptic traditions. Specific rabbis are known to have taught mystical theology and practice in the first centuries CE. Some
scholars think that the Gnostics of the early Christian era (ca.
100–200 CE) developed their ideas from a core Jewish mystical tradition that existed before the first century. We have
Jewish mystical texts that date back, in their first written forms,
to the second or third century CE, and possibly earlier, but we
know very little about the transmission and interpretation of
these texts in that period. From the fascinating teachings that
have come down to us, it is highly likely that the mystics limited their teachings to small circles because they were concerned about being considered culturally and even politically
subversive in a variety of ways.[1] Yet in the long run, their
thought was highly influential. The traditional Jewish prayer
book, first compiled and circulated in writing in the eighth
century CE, incorporates profound mystical ideas.

Whatever the reasons for the original secrecy, Kabbalah in a variety of interpretations became better known in the Middle Ages, even though its teachers still emphasized oral, teacher-to-student transmission. Among the best-known works circulating among the mystical masters of Europe were the *Sefer Yetzirah* (the oldest known Jewish mystical work, probably second century) and the *Bahir* (eleventh century). Major schools of mysticism existed in Germanic territory, in southern France, and in Spain, where the famous *Zohar* was published in the late 1200s. A very important biblical commentator of the same period, Moshe ben Nachman (Nachmanides) was one of the Spanish mystics; he frequently refers to mystical teachings in his commentary. It was probably no accident that these developments paralleled the growth of mysticism in medieval Christianity, from the Marianic devotion of Bernard of Clairvaux in the early twelfth century to the more philosophical mysticism of Meister Eckhart in the late thirteenth century.

A couple of centuries later, after Spain expelled its Jews in 1492, mysticism traveled with the exiles to Italy, the Balkans, and the Land of Israel. By the mid-sixteenth century, a number of outstanding scholars and mystics had settled in Safed (pronounced *ts'faht*), a small town in the Galil (northern Israel). Their presence attracted more individuals with similar inclinations, and soon Safed became the world center of Jewish mystical piety. When a remarkable rabbi named Isaac Luria arrived there in 1569, he quickly became the acknowledged master of the group and spent the next three years, until his death, consolidating, explaining, and elaborating the mystical heritage. Lurianic mysticism became the basis for much of Jewish mysticism down to the present day.

Political and economic changes led to the decline of Safed in the next century, but the teachings emerging from that center continued to engage the interest of the devout. The next great eruption of mysticism came in the form of a popular movement in the 1660s led by Shabbatai Tzvi, an erratic teacher whose disciples believed him to be the Messiah, but who converted to Islam to escape death. After that debacle, many rabbis discouraged the teaching of mysticism to the general populace and invoked again the traditional prescription of secrecy. Great mystics were carefully watched and sometimes forbidden to publicize their teachings. For example, nearly a hundred years later, Rabbi Moshe Chaim Luzzato (1707–1746) taught a devoted group of disciples in Italy, but when contemporary rabbinic leaders learned that Luzzato believed some of his students to be incarnations of past great leaders, and one to be a potential messiah, he was forbidden to teach. He moved to Amsterdam but again met with discouragement. Nevertheless, a number of Luzzato's works gained acceptance and are today much respected in the history of mysticism.[2]

Many mystics stayed underground. According to one tradition, a circle known as the "hidden ones" carried on the teachings of Rabbi Isaac Luria for nearly two hundred years in Eastern Europe. In 1740, a member of this circle emerged into public view in the Ukraine, saying that it was now time to reinvigorate mystical teachings among the general populace. Though his given name was Israel ben Eliezer, he is known in history as the Baal Shem Tov—"Master of the Good Name." His teachings, transmitted by his disciples and theirs in turn, sparked flames of piety across Eastern Europe.

The members of this movement were known as Hasidim (or Chassidim), meaning "the devout ones." They taught love of God, joy in worship, and the ability of every Jew to be connected to God through prayer and service, whether or not a person was learned according to rabbinic criteria. Although this way of transmitting mystical teachings also had opponents, Hasidism grew to become a major influence on the piety of the Jews of Eastern Europe. Interestingly, this movement was emerging at the same time as pietistic devotion in Protestant Christianity—Pietism among German Lutherans, Methodism among Anglicans in England, and the Great Awakening in the American colonies.

In addition, many great non-Hasidic scholars continued to study Kabbalah. In the nineteenth century, even among the non-Hasidic groups, a young man who showed intellectual promise and a desire to inquire into esoteric meanings might be given a copy of the *Zohar*—one of the classic mystical texts—when he was still a teenager.[3] Mysticism continued to be studied, even while the Reform movement among German Jews espoused a rationalist, largely antimystical position. Unfortunately, persecutions and pogroms in late-nineteenth-century Russia decimated many of the traditional Jewish communities where the mystics were nourished. Most dramatically, in the Holocaust perpetrated by Nazi Germany in the mid-twentieth century, 90 percent of Eastern Europe's rabbis were slaughtered. Still, Hasidic traditions and some of the masters of Hasidic teachings survived and brought their message to the United States, in waves of immigration that began at the end of the nineteenth century.

Until the 1950s, access to the traditions was confined mostly to the Orthodox enclaves of major cities, for all the Hasidim were Orthodox, as were Sephardic Jews who also maintained strong mystical traditions. Traditional Hasidic tales and sayings became known to the educated public largely through the work of Martin Buber, originally from a Hasidic tradition, although he had left observance behind. In the early 1970s, a sea change began as the Lubavitch sect of Hasidim known as Chabad (tracing its roots to the town of Lubavitch in Russia) began campaigns to spread knowledge of basic Jewish practices and Hasidic teachings to assimilated and non-

Orthodox American Jews. Both through its official rabbinic representatives and through teachers who were trained in Chabad but left the confines of the group, mystical teachings became far more accessible, even to Jews uneducated in the tradition. The Jewish Renewal movement, which attracted young Jews in major cities beginning in the 1970s, encouraged serious study of mysticism as well as other aspects of Jewish tradition. By the end of the twentieth century, a wide variety of Jewish groups included mysticism, at least occasionally, as part of their teachings.

Meanwhile, the American public had demonstrated a growing interest in spirituality since the 1960s, an interest that increased dramatically in the 1990s. Most of that interest was at first directed toward Eastern thought, especially Hinduism and Buddhism, or to theosophical and occult traditions that had previously been of interest only to an elite minority. But non-Jews also became interested in Kabbalah. This was not entirely a new development. As we will see in Chapter 1, non-Jews have sought spiritual insight from kabbalistic traditions before. But as awareness of Kabbalah spread through the mass media, popular interest in Kabbalah grew larger than ever.

At present, different approaches to Kabbalah are available. In Orthodox Hasidism, as well as in neo-Hasidic groups that do not stress observance of Jewish law, mystical interpretations are incorporated as part of general Jewish learning. Studying mystical teachings while learning the Bible, prayer, and Jewish law is the most integrated approach. But, for the non-Jewish beginner with a strong interest in mysticism, such an avenue is very difficult because it requires familiarity with many basic Jewish texts and concepts, and often with Hebrew words and letters. Another recently emerging alternative is groups that specialize in Kabbalah for a general audience, but one must be careful because some of these groups are of doubtful authenticity and/or use questionable methods to gain adherents. Yet another way is reading books by non-Jewish kabbalists, but most of these are interlaced with intricate esoteric interpretations from other theosophical traditions and do not present Jewish Kabbalah in a straightforward manner. Finally, in very recent times a number of writers, including myself, have begun the effort of making the concepts of mystical Judaism available for the general reader. This book in particular is intended to make some of this knowledge more readily accessible to Christian readers, in hopes of encouraging dialogue among spiritual practitioners in both faiths.

PART I

SEEKING A NEW VISION

1

OPENING THE WORLD
OF KABBALAH

Let them make Me a dwelling place,
that I may dwell among them.

—EXODUS 25:8

FROM CONCEALMENT TO REVELATION

A HIDDEN TRADITION. Esoteric, complicated, dangerous. Only
a few could study it, and it was carefully guarded from the
unlearned and outsiders.

This is the reputation of Kabbalah, as the ancient tradition
of Jewish mysticism is known. Today, however, its basic teachings are available to the general educated public. Movie stars
study Kabbalah. You can pick up at your local bookstore
numerous introductions to its basic vocabulary and conceptual
structure. Other books offer insights on Jewish meditation.
Academic works purport to reveal the psychology or social
history of mysticism.

Yet if you think about it, this sudden accessibility is a
little suspicious. If Kabbalah was so secret for so long, how can
we approach it so easily now? If it is so difficult, how can it be
made simple enough for a popular audience? And if it has been
around for millennia, why is it coming to the fore at this time?
Is there something special about the resurgence of Jewish

mystical tradition among the many religious theories and many forms of meditation and self-improvement available today?

Kabbalah has been hidden to a considerable degree, and the fact that it is coming into public vision now is no accident. The Jewish mystics have taught that although all spiritual teaching goes back to the original divine revelation encapsulated at Mount Sinai (Exod. 20), the particular form in which a teaching appears is appropriate to its era and its audience. As the ancient Rabbis taught in a *midrash* (a story handed down to explain a biblical text), God provides the remedy before the disease. The appearance of Kabbalah in public means that Jewish mysticism has something unique to offer, a power for healing the spirit as we move into a radically new future.

Many thinkers now acknowledge that the dominant thought systems of the modern West—particularly extreme rationalism and overzealous faith in science—no longer are sufficient to nourish human and planetary life. As a result, various forms of ancient spirituality, formerly esoteric and inaccessible, are now being translated into terms comprehensible to a popular audience. We do not yet know exactly how to do this translation. Some of the richness of complex traditions like Kabbalah is undoubtedly lost in the process of popularization. But if the wisdom of the core teachings can be preserved and transmitted, the tradeoff is worthwhile. This wisdom can be particularly valuable if the teachings can be shared across the boundaries that have marked our different traditions—in the present case, Judaism and Christianity. The enrichment we receive from others will help us—collective humanity—to rethink and re-imagine our world and our personal lives along spiritual lines.

Kabbalah offers truly unique insights that enable us to probe into the realities of the world. Moreover, it presents its truths in an expansive and unusually comprehensive framework. Many books talk about holistic perspectives, but

Kabbalah makes clear that holism must be integrated with an appreciation of plurality and diversity. It also insists that we view our personal journeys in the larger context of what is happening in God's world, for that is the only way to avoid creating another mystical narcissism.

This book will provide you with guideposts in understanding Kabbalah. As you absorb the lessons of Jewish mysticism, you will be able to think in new ways—as a citizen of the cosmos as well as a member of your own faith—and align your life more expansively with the greatest spiritual aspirations of humankind.

REMEMBERING WHO WE ARE

Let's start with a basic question: Why is it that human beings encounter so many problems in life? Why are we beset with war and racism, political and ethnic conflicts, disharmony with our environment, and shattering events in our personal lives? Kabbalah tells us that the ultimate cause of our problems, from our personal lives to the widest range of humanity, is forgetting who we are. We have forgotten our true selves and our true purpose.[1]

This teaching brings us some good news: In our deepest core, we do know who we are. When we rediscover it, we will recognize it because it is not alien to us. This teaching comes ultimately from the Bible, which clearly states that human beings are made in the divine image—that is who we truly are. Our purpose is to become clear mirrors of divinity. Sometimes we see glimpses of our true inner selves, our divine selves. But most of the time, in our haze of half-knowing, we create layer upon layer of delusion about our lives.

Jewish teachings are somewhat different from Christian ones on this issue. Most Christian traditions emphasize the

5

sinful nature of humanity—sin being understood as rebellion, pride, or corruption. Judaism certainly recognizes such traits in human nature but tends to focus on other aspects: misunderstanding, misperception, ignorance. A famous saying from the rabbinic tradition is that a person sins out of foolishness: If we only recognized the consequences of our actions and thoughts, we would not sin! The view here (and not necessarily a universally held one, since Judaism is not monolithic) is that sinful traits are not so embedded in our nature that we cannot overcome them. Of course, understanding and choosing correctly is not easy because there are so many dimensions of delusion, error, and wrongheadedness.

The Jewish mystics add another twist to this perspective. They say that our misunderstanding, based in our "forgetting" of our divine origin, is actually necessary so that God's purpose in creating the earth can be accomplished. If we truly remembered accurately and clearly why we are here, we would not have free choice. We would be like angels who simply perform, without doubt or ambivalence, the duties assigned to them. But if we are truly to manifest godliness, we cannot be programmed into our assignments, because one of the characteristics of being made in the divine image is the ability to create freely. Thus, paradoxically, by obscuring our origins, God was able to give us free choice—to choose whether or not to manifest as loving, creative images of the Divine. This is simply the nature of earthly existence according to Kabbalah, and many other forms of mysticism agree. We volunteered for earthly service, but part of the package is that we cannot remember doing so. That is what makes life such a challenge.

Along with forgetting who we are come other problems: self-doubt and insecurity. Our uncertainty about what we are doing here distorts everything in our culture. We live in a time when human beings have achieved more than people of previous centuries could even dream. On the surface, we appear to be self-confident, assured creatures. But our culture reveals the opposite: Books, newspaper columns, talk shows, and self-help groups constantly address the issue of self-esteem. Group rivalry and ethnic conflict escalate to shore up weak social identities. Why are we so insecure? To use an image from Christian scripture, we have built our houses on sand instead of rock. The sand is the idea that we are separate, independent individuals, desperately competing in an alien world. The rock is our connection to God. When we are not in touch with the ultimate source that can give us a picture of our true worth, we will slip and slide into the sea of false knowledge that inundates our information age. What we need is not only the deep knowledge of ourselves as truly created in the image of God, but also the experience of ourselves as profoundly connected to each other and to the rest of creation.

The idea that we are made in the image of God is such an awesome thought that we hide it from ourselves. The great modern Jewish philosopher Abraham Joshua Heschel wrote sadly, "The man of today shrinks from the light."[2] We may want to believe we are made in the divine image, but then we undermine ourselves by saying, "We can't really know God. So what good is it anyway?" Judaism says clearly that we must each take on the responsibility to engage with God and the world in the ways God has revealed to us. Moreover, through spiritual practice guided by the wisdom of Torah—more than three thousand years of oral and written traditions about God's revelation—we can develop the ability to understand the higher teachings of mysticism and ultimately to manifest godliness.

Kabbalah is the discipline that teaches us directly about godliness, about divinity as we can relate to it in our lives. Scholars have called it a "theosophy," which means "wisdom about the Divine." Only when we have a grasp on the meaning of divinity and divine purpose can we possibly understand what we are here for. Intellectual work is thus an important part of Kabbalah. If we ask questions and are told "you just have to accept it," that's insufficient. We can't just recite words and phrases that are meaningless to us. Traditional religious virtues like faith and trust are important categories in Judaism generally and in Kabbalah in particular, but we must also be willing to embark on a journey that will stretch the mind.

Are there reasons to avoid the study of mystical traditions like Kabbalah? Religious authorities have sometimes believed that esoteric wisdom is dangerous to the social order, because religious enthusiasm could often be manipulated by the unscrupulous (as indeed it has been). Historically, mysticism has also been seen as dangerous to those in power, as mystics who believed in the divine image in everyone have tended to be concerned about equity and justice. But these are all reflections of the tendencies of institutions to protect themselves. Mysticism is in fact a creative force that helps transform institutions in spiritual and ethical ways.

According to Jewish mysticism, all of us have the gifts we need to reflect the image of God, each in our own unique way. The very fact that we have arrived here, in human incarnation, tells us that we have the courage to take on the task. Today, although we are busy and often preoccupied with day-to-day matters, many of us actively desire to have our entire lives permeated with spirituality. We want to work at creating our lives around a higher ideal. The teachings of Kabbalah are appropriate because Kabbalah was not cultivated in a "saintly" atmosphere completely separate from daily life. Most rabbis, including many kabbalists, worked for a living at some trade or business. If they wanted to be close to God, they had to commit time and energy to it, but most had to do it while they were living a normal life. Hasidic teachings in particular insist, with traditional Judaism, that our "temple" is the home as well as the synagogue or religious institution; that marrying and raising children is just as holy as having a separate spiritual life; that caring for our bodies and minds is as important as spiritual experience.

Of course, special times and activities such as retreats and purifications can be helpful as part of a spiritual practice. Mystics in Judaism as in other traditions were known to depart from the normal person's routine—for example, by sleeping less or fasting more. But Judaism holds that, for most people, separations from the world should be temporary and limited, enabling us to refresh our connection to spirit. We must then return to the world and integrate what we have received. This is the point of our effort, for the ultimate goal is that *the whole world will become a vessel for divinity.* When humans reach the point of "From my flesh I will see God!" as Job says (19:26), the purpose of creation will be realized. We will have remembered and fully realized our divine image.

Kabbalah provides a unique system for enabling us to do this. It continually tries to point us to the deeper levels of everything we do. Nothing in the world is outside its purview. Kabbalah teaches, for example, that our true divine purpose can never be completely forgotten. If we look with a compassionate eye at our lives and at the society we live in, we can perceive that most people are indeed striving for spiritual greatness but have expressed that striving only in partial, truncated ways. Science's quest for power over nature, an individual's aspiration for wealth and honor, our desperate searches for love and pleasure are all part of the same effort. They are all part of divinity—love, power, honor, and delight are all attributes of God. But in our society they are usually cut off from their ultimate source, so they do not give full satisfaction.

For Kabbalah, everything is a metaphor that provides access to ultimate reality. Problems that arise on one level can be resolved on another. And at each point, we are thrown back to the question "How can we manifest godliness? How can we be divine?"

IS KABBALAH ONLY FOR JEWS?

God isn't only for Jews, so neither is Kabbalah. While there are some aspects of Kabbalah that are almost impossible to understand without absorbing a great deal of Jewish tradition, Kabbalah as a theosophy is primarily about understanding what God is (as far as humans can understand) and who we are as refractions of the divine image. Because of this, it is important for all peoples.

Yet, according to the popular conception among Jews, you couldn't study Kabbalah unless you were forty years old, married, and male—and, traditionally, Jewish. What these criteria meant was that a student should be mature, well grounded in the basics of Judaism (including the rich oral tradition of commentary known as Talmud), and stable in his personal life. Because a strong grounding in biblical and Talmudic texts was presupposed, women were not included. Women were taught the portions of Torah necessary to live a Jewish life, which was a considerable amount of learning, but they generally did not have access to Talmudic learning or extensive biblical commentaries. Rules also restricted certain kinds of kabbalistic interpretation and use of divine names. All these restrictions would apply to non-Jews even more.

There were good reasons for the restrictions. If one studied kabbalistic texts without an appropriate background, one could easily misinterpret them. An uneducated interpreter would be like a person trying to fill a doctor's prescription without going to pharmaceutical school—even if you could read the writing, you wouldn't understand the code. Nevertheless, restrictions on some teachings were gradually lifted beginning around the twelfth century, and writings of masters of Kabbalah slowly became accessible to the literate Jewish population. At certain periods in the Middle Ages, mystical teachings began to spread more widely—although that did not mean, in medieval and early modern times, what it does today. When books had to be copied painstakingly by hand, they were expensive and scarce. The writings of the mystical masters were more difficult than biblical Hebrew, and some were in Aramaic. Even after the printing revolution of the sixteenth century, the literate Jewish population who could read those languages well was largely limited to males. The subject matter of the mystical writings was highly esoteric, including many intricate interpretations of Hebrew letters and words and their numerical value. Nevertheless, over the centuries and especially through oral traditions, the general concepts of Jewish mysticism gradually became available to those who sought them. The concepts of medieval Kabbalah were familiar to some Christian scholars and mystics. By the time of the Renaissance, those teachings were regarded as part of the general heritage of Western mysticism. Kabbalah was also influential in the theosophical movements that emerged in nineteenth-century Europe and North America, which in turn have influenced contemporary spirituality.

In short, Kabbalah in the general sense has not always been limited to Jews, and some of the basic concepts of Kabbalah, such as we will study in this book, can be understood without an extensive Jewish education. More intricate teachings are difficult to access from outside Judaism, and it is probably wise to be suspicious of anyone who says they are teaching deep mysteries to people without a background in

Judaism. Nevertheless, opening up the insights of the ancient mystics can be a significant step. By learning something about Kabbalah, you can deepen your insight into the highest teachings of your own tradition.

HOW KABBALAH CAN HELP YOU

Kabbalah is exciting because it is multidimensional. Ever since I began my studies with rabbis from Hasidic traditions that were shaped by Kabbalah, I was fascinated by its conceptual structure. Soon I learned that people in these traditions were practicing various forms of meditation, which I had thought was only for Hindus and Buddhists. At the same time, I saw an intense devotion to what I had always loved about Judaism, namely, an insistence on applying spirituality to practical action in the world. As I continued my own studies, I discovered teachings about physical health, emotional development, childhood education, and relationships. And in each case I found that when my teachers explained the issue in depth, they were drawing me back to that single focus: Bring God into the world. You and I, each one of us personally, has the job of making the world a place where God can dwell. That task goes on daily, nightly, weekly, yearly. All of us, collectively, are creating the body of God.[3] The task is awesome and challenging, and at the same time delightful and deeply meaningful.

That task is what I want to introduce to you in the chapters that follow. Kabbalah is a theology that gives rise to a cosmology and an anthropology. As a theology, it presents God as active, in dynamic interaction with the created world. As a cosmology, it shows how the world emanates from God. As an anthropology, it is a map of humanity in our effort to approach the Divine and to bring divinity into our corner of the cosmos—to "make a dwelling place" for God, as we were commanded in the Book of Exodus. In Chapter 2, I will offer an overall perspective of this cosmology and anthropology and introduce the basic vocabulary that we will use. This vocabulary may not be familiar at first, but will become almost second nature by the time you reach the end of the book. Several alternative translations of the Hebrew terminology are in use; I have adapted them to convey, as best as possible, the various levels of divine manifestation that Kabbalah is trying to express.

Then, in Part II, we will examine in greater detail the kabbalistic map of divinity, the way that God expresses Godself in the world. I call this "The Unfolding of Creation." The three chapters in this section look at the kabbalistic Tree of Life from the top down. A fascinating aspect of this side of our study is that kabbalistic teachings seem to run parallel to some of today's advanced scientific cosmologies, and I will allude to some of these parallels.

Kabbalah involves not only study and contemplation of the Divine, but also self-reflection and prayer to incorporate this knowledge into our own lives. In order to accomplish this, we must review our personal and collective history in light of the Kabbalah's anthropology. I call this process the "Path of Remembering," and describe it in Part III. In these three chapters, we will reexamine the kabbalistic map, with its segments considered in reverse order from the study of creation. This will enable you to look at your personal life, from birth to the present, to see how it can be understood as part of an unfolding spiritual path.

While we will focus on understanding, it is important to remember that Kabbalah is implicitly a path of action, one that enables us to transform the world. The traditional prescription of divine commandments, whether for Jews or non-Jews, have been understood in Kabbalah to be expressions of a divine embodiment in the world.[4] The Hebrew word for commandment, *mitzvah,* is related to an ancient root that means "connection." We connect to our divine source by doing certain acts and abstaining from others. It is not that an external force demands obedience from us; rather, we know deeply, inwardly, that something calls us to a higher way of life. As the Torah says, "It is very near to you, in your mouth and in your heart to do it" (Deut. 30:14). Although we will not undertake the study of commandments in this book, we must remember that through certain kinds of action and nonaction, we express the divine will that wants to be acting through us and thus enables us to join in the divine delight that comes from uniting act and intent, spiritual consciousness and physical reality.

The path of Kabbalah is a wondrous journey. It's one I've been pursuing for nearly thirty years, and I'm still fascinated by each facet of life that is illuminated by integrating this mode of study and practice into my life. I hope that this introduction to Kabbalah will affect your experience of life, so that you will find it easier to look beyond appearances and go beneath the surface of things. Ultimately, I hope you will see clearly that we all are vessels for divine energy, not only a reflection of the divine image, but also potentially co-creators with God.

2

KABBALAH AND THE IMAGE OF GOD

A procession of angels passes before each person, and the
heralds go before them, saying, "Make way for the image
of the Holy One Blessed-Be-He!"

—*DEUTERONOMY RABBA* 4:4

WHERE IS THE REAL WORLD?

A GREAT RABBI of one of the European schools of learning said
that the greatest secrets of Kabbalah are secrets only until they
are known. Once you understand them, they are as simple and
open as the palm of your hand.

This is true of the first basic principle of Kabbalah: *The
world we see is not the real world.* More precisely, the world *as we
see it* is not the real world. Kabbalah does not hold, as some
Eastern religious systems do, that the world is an illusion; however, our sight is limited. This is no secret—it is an obvious
truth. We know from astronomy and microbiology that the
world is much larger and more complex than it appears at first
sight. In addition, all the inventions we have created to expand
the range of our senses, from microscopes to radar telescopes,
are also limited. The world that we can perceive is a mere slice
of a multidimensional world beyond our senses and even
beyond our mathematics.

In Kabbalah we learn that the world is a partial manifestation of a much larger ultimate reality, which we call God. The kabbalists called that reality *Ein Sof,* "There Is No End" or, more simply, the Infinite. The aspect of God that is reflected in our cosmos is the Light of the Infinite.

Perhaps the idea that God is infinite appears to be an obvious truth as well. In the Western world it is customary to refer to God as the Creator, and multitudes believe that an all-powerful entity we call God created the world, in one way or another. But here we are saying something a little bit different. The *Tanya,* a classic book of modern mysticism, expresses it in this way: The Blessed Holy One is not separate from creation even for a moment. God's light, which is "part" of the infinite God, is immanent in everything everywhere always.

Some contemporary thinkers explain this by using the metaphor of a hologram to describe the relation of the created universe to its source in the Divine. A hologram is a picture taken by laser light that has certain peculiar properties. When exposed on the appropriate kind of photographic film, the hologram shows the full picture of the object in three dimensions. If you cut the film in half, each half will also show the full picture of the object in three dimensions, unlike a normal photo, which if cut in half shows only the top half in one slice and the bottom in the other. In a holographic image, the only difference from the original will be that the half-picture is slightly less focused than the whole one. If you continue snipping the film into smaller and smaller pieces, each tiny piece will still contain the image of the entire original object. However, the smaller the pieces are, the fuzzier they will be.

In this metaphor, the laser light is God's light projecting an image of God, and the created universe is the picture or hologram representing God. Each entity within the universe is one of the snippets of film. Each contains *all* the elements of divine manifestation (for which we will learn the terms later on). All of God is included in any part of creation. Thus the holographic image, though separate from the original, contains all the information that the original contained.

However, the fuzziness means it is not always equally easy to see God. God's signature may not be so clear in a piece of gravel from the driveway, for example. We may think it is clearer in a rainbow, or in a sunset over the ocean; and it may radiate more to us through a newborn baby than in our next-door neighbor. Nevertheless, each is its own refraction of divinity.

The fact that reality is a refraction of God's light provides us with our religious metaphors. A piece of rock may represent one metaphor for God—indeed, religious texts like the Prophets and Psalms sometimes describe God as a rock, inviting us to imagine God's firmness, strength, and immovability. When we speak of God's purity, however, we might use the image of the fresh innocence of a newborn baby. God offers us metaphors for divinity in every aspect of our lives. We can see them if we look.

At the same time, we must recognize that our finite minds cannot comprehend in any precise way the relation between God and creation. Perhaps the best we can say is that the universe is God unfolding him-her-itself. All the information we have about the world—the mirror image of yourself in the mirror, the feelings you have as you greet the sun in the morning, the latest scientific theory you read about in the newspaper—are shadows or holographic snapshots or metaphors of God. They make up our universe, which is constantly expanding as we get more pictures.

One of the names for God in the Bible is "I will be what I will be." This implies that God is in the process of manifesting in the world. Still, much of God is concealed, and according to Kabbalah, there are different levels of manifestation and concealment. While every entity in the universe is constructed of the divine elements, not all those elements are manifest in every being. Stones do not reveal life force, for example, and plants do not demonstrate mobility. The human being is called in the Bible "the divine image" because Adam, the first (male/female) human being, and all his/her descendants revealed the greatest possible range of divine attributes on earth.

As a result each human being, without exception, carries the stamp of divinity. With all our differences, even being split into six billion people incarnated on this planet, each of us is still a complete hologram of God.

The only problem is, like the tiny holographic photo, each of us is somewhat fuzzy. It's hard to see God's image clearly. Because it is blurry, some of our divine nature is, as Kabbalah terms it, concealed. That concealment presents us with our life task: to become "revealed," to be a clear, radiant image of the Divine.

THE TURKEY PRINCE

Unfortunately, the world in its present state does not tell us we are divine or that our life work is to radiate divinity. Instead, its regular and repeated message is that we are poor, struggling creatures who must compete to survive and acquire as much as we can. A famous story from a Hasidic master, Rabbi Nachman of Breslov, illustrates this point.

> A royal prince once became mad and thought that he was a turkey. He felt compelled to sit naked under the table, pecking at bones and pieces of bread like a turkey. The royal physicians gave up hope of ever curing him of his madness, and his father, the king, suffered tremendous grief.
>
> A sage then came and said, "I will undertake to cure him."

The sage undressed and sat naked under the table next to the prince, pecking at crumbs and bones. "Who are you?" asked the prince. "What are you doing here?"

"And you?" replied the sage. "What are you doing here?"

"I am a turkey," said the prince.

"I am also a turkey," answered the sage.

They sat together like this for some time, until they became good friends. One day, the sage signaled the king's servants to throw him shirts. He said to the prince, "What makes you think that a turkey can't wear a shirt? You can wear a shirt and still be a turkey." With that, the two of them put on shirts.

After a while, the sage signaled the servants again, and they threw him a pair of pants. Just as before, he said, "What makes you think that you can't be a turkey if you wear pants?"

The sage continued in this manner until they were both completely dressed. Then he signaled again, and they were given regular food from the table. Again the sage said, "What makes you think that you will stop being a turkey if you eat good food? You can eat whatever you want and still be a turkey!" They both ate the food.

Finally the sage said, "What makes you think that a turkey has to sit under the table? Even a turkey can sit at the table."

The sage continued in this manner until the prince was completely cured.[1]

The turkey prince is a metaphor for each of our lives. You can probably think of many times when you realized you were so narrowly focused on getting what you wanted that you missed seeing something beautiful or appreciating someone in your life. This narrow-mindedness is part of the human condition. We spend most of our time going after things that we think will satisfy us, but we don't even notice the great palace of our beautiful planet, or the banquet table of gifts set before us. We do not know that we are truly royalty, made in the divine image. We are governed by our lower appetites— what the mystics call our animal souls—and cannot see beyond our immediate needs and pleasures.

Collectively, we are completely immersed in a narrow version of reality. Even if we were able to peek out above the tablecloth, we would probably only see the beautiful silver and crystal on the table. A few of us might be so tuned in that we could hear the conversations going on among the nobility. A very tiny group might be able to gaze around and see the intricate designs of the tapestries or glimpse the architecture of the palace beyond. But almost all of us would miss the most beautiful sight of all—the radiance of the loving face that belongs to the king, the owner of the palace, court, and banquet. Yet this is the goal. As an early Christian theologian wrote of God, "He starts to be revealed clearly and to be known in a great familiarity and to be seen more clearly, the invisible, invisibly speaks and hears and, as if a friend to a friend, face to face."[2]

The yearning to be close to God—what the Hasidic masters call *devekut* or clinging ("To Him you shall cling," Deut. 10:20)—is expressed in a beautiful hymn sung by traditional Jews near the opening and closing of the holy Shabbat, the seventh day of the week (sunset Friday till dark on Saturday evening), which celebrates God's creating and blessing the world.

> Beloved of my soul, compassionate Father, draw me, Your
>   servant, toward your pleasure.
> Your servant will run like a doe and bow before your beauty!
> Sweeter will Your love be than the dripping honeycomb, or
>   any taste.

Beautiful, delightful, Radiance of the universe—my soul is
lovesick for You!
Please, God, heal her now by showing her the pleasure of
Your radiance,
Then she will be strengthened and healed and will experi-
ence eternal joy.

Ancient One, arouse your mercy, please, and take pity on
the child of Your beloved,
For it is so long I have yearned and longed to see soon the
splendor of Your power.
This is the desire of my heart, so please take pity and do not
hide!

Reveal Yourself, please, and spread over me, my Beloved, the
shelter of Your peace!
Illuminate the earth with Your glory, and we will be glad
and rejoice in You!
Hasten, show love, for the time is come, and be gracious to
us as in days of old.

On Shabbat, the Jewish people enter into the reality of the
palace and the King's table. The rest of the week, we coax ourselves into integrating that grander perspective only a little bit
at a time, like the prince putting on the royal garments one by
one. Kabbalah, too, asks us to proceed step by step, trying on
each garment and getting used to it. The wise man waved no
magic wand, nor did he teach the prince to chant mystical
words to be free from his affliction. Patiently, he helped him
work his way into it, until he was cured of his narrow delusions.

And, the prince did not have to give up what he wanted
to be. He could still be a turkey as long as he wanted. Each of
us has our own nature, which will not be overruled but rather

transformed. From a childhood version of who we want to be—an astronaut, a police officer, a doctor, or a turkey—we build our ideals. From the apparent accidents of our birth, our family, our traumas and successes, our unique form emerges, yearning to be filled with higher purpose. The idiosyncrasies that mark our specialness, even the mysterious aspects of ourselves, will all come to fruition in ways we cannot imagine, in our ultimate spiritual reality.

REVEALING DIVINE LIGHT

The prince (or princess) is the divine image within each of us. The King, of course, is God. The effort to get up from under the table is our striving toward the essential godliness, the uniqueness of our God-given soul, that each of us deeply desires to manifest so that we can be close to God. The scriptures say, "Be holy as I am holy" (Lev. 11:44). This is similar to the message of many traditions, that the goal of the human being is to be like God or to imitate someone who reached nearly divine heights.

The biblical creation story tells us that we started out being godlike; human beings were made "in the image of God." But Adam and Eve were also vulnerable to the wily words of the Garden's strange serpent. Even though everything they were experiencing was "very good," he persuaded them that eating the fruit of the forbidden tree would make them more like God. Jewish teachings suggest also that they became impatient and were not willing to wait for God's next communication—which would have ushered them into the culminating beauty of Shabbat. Instead of listening to God and maintaining their relationship with the Divine, they listened to their desires and were overcome by doubt and confusion. Since then, we have had great difficulty in holding onto our compass for divinity.

In a sense, Adam and Eve were too uncertain, too fragile to hold the divine glory. That sense of fragility echoes a kabbalistic explanation of the creation story. According to the master kabbalist of sixteenth-century Safed, Rabbi Isaac Luria (1520–1572), the divine light gave form to the world by emanating ten vessels, or *sefirot* (pronounced *suh-fee-ROAT*), and then pouring light into them. But the original light was too powerful, and it shattered the vessels, scattering shards of light throughout the universe. Those shards make up our present world. Each shard is now covered with a *klipah,* or shell, and the human task is to crack open the shell to reveal the light. The shell is the façade; the light inside is true being. On the human level, the shell is our persona or ego, the front we show to the world. The light inside is our soul, our unique refraction of the divine image.

The task—the correction for the original error of Adam and Eve—is to separate the good and evil that have been mixed in the world. This separation happens every time we make a choice for the good. Yet, Kabbalah teaches, we do not merely make a series of good choices, as though we have a checklist in front of us through our lives. This would be rather disheartening, since our choices are so numerous that we could hardly be confident of making them all correctly. Rather, as we choose the good, we also begin to re-create ourselves as beings that shine with an inner light. We can become more and more in tune with our divine source so that our daily choices come from the pure core of our being. For Judaism teaches that every soul is pure in essence; there is no incorrigible flaw in any soul.

We can imagine each human as a beautiful old lamp into which a rich, shining oil is poured, so it looks like a rainbow filling the vessel. But the lantern is crusted over and nearly full of a coarse brown sediment. Once the oil is inside, you cannot see it at all because of the dark residue. If you start spooning out the sediment and cleaning the inner surface, you will begin to see the radiant oil even though sediment remains on the bottom. The more you spoon out and clear away, the more of the liquid you will be able to see. This is a gradual process of refinement that suggests a way to do spiritual work. When we discover something is blocking our manifestation of the divine image, we clear it out, and more of our true inner light can shine. The metaphor of refinement is similar to one used by the fifteenth-century Christian theologian Thomas à Kempis, who wrote: "As iron cast into fire loses its rust and becomes glowing white, so he who turns completely to God is stripped of his sluggishness and changed into a new man."[3]

Yet even as we contemplate this possibility of refining ourselves, we ask whether it is possible. Can we really overturn our turkey habits and become royalty, filled with divine purpose? Society often reinforces our inner fear that only a rare individual can be God-filled, by sanctifying certain types of people and ignoring others. But it is not true! Please erase from your inner tapes the belief that only certain people can achieve closeness to God or unification with their true divine image. An ordinary person, rooted in daily life, can do this. We need only to fill our own life with the light of goodness. Just as a shoe is formed on a last, we need only follow the shape of our own soul.

Fortunately, we have help in discovering that shape. We have a map that will guide us through the territory of the soul, the map that has been called the Tree of Life.

MAPPING THE DIVINE ENERGIES

The ordinary world is really only the lowest level—"under the table"—of a great cosmic palace. Similarly, human beings are not simply what we appear to be. We are not equivalent to our physical bodies, for example. The bodies we experience are dense manifestations of a deeper structure known as the Tree of Life or

Tree of the *Sefirot*. As we saw above, *sefirot* is the term for the original vessels into which divine light was poured. Although those original vessels were shattered, their form was reconstructed and became the basic template for the next creation that ensued.

The concept of *sefirot* is unfamiliar, in this form, to most Christians, so let me explain it a little more. The earliest references we have are in the *Sefer Yetzirah*, an ancient set of teachings that appears to have been known in written form no later than the third century CE. It speaks several times of the "Ten *Sefirot* of Nothingness" and describes them as follows:

> Their measure is ten that have no end—
> A depth of beginning, a depth of end,
> A depth of good, a depth of evil,
> A depth of above, a depth of below,
> A depth of east, a depth of west,
> A depth of north, a depth of south,
> The unique Master, God faithful King, rules over them all ...[4]

The commentaries explain that these *sefirot* allude to attributes and names of God. Indeed, the *Sefer Yetzirah* opens a few verses earlier with an accolade to God the Creator, using ten different biblical expressions for God. This is not far from ancient Christian teachings, which were well aware of the significance of divine attributes; for example, the influential fourth-century theologian who wrote under the name of Dionysius the Areopagite composed a lengthy treatise on the divine names.[5]

In time, the import of the other biblical names faded from Christian memory except in ritual formulas such as "In the name of the Father and of the Son and of the Holy Spirit." But in Kabbalah, their significance was kept alive. The "names" were understood as the ways in which God has chosen to manifest divinity in the world, and knowledge of their inner meaning was a key, both to closeness to God and to bringing God's plan to fruition. By medieval times, the mystery of divine names had achieved expression in the diagram of ten *sefirot*, which may have originally been an attempt to chart the ten "depths" alluded to in *Sefer Yetzirah*.

In kabbalistic language then, if we speak of the *sefirah* (singular form) of *Tiferet*-Splendor, we mean that God manifests in the world through what we perceive as splendor, which we often associate with extraordinary beauty or harmony. The word *splendor* attempts to grasp something of that particular mode of God's self-revelation. But we should not be too attached to the precise wording, for the divine name associated with splendor is far deeper than the English word. The words merely point in the direction of something that must be discovered in deeper investigation.

The difficulty of capturing God's manifestation in words tells us that the *sefirot* also represent levels of concealment. Kabbalah teaches that the divine light is so intense that if it were presented to us directly, we could not see it at all—in fact, we could not exist. As we saw, in a previous creation the vessels were shattered by the intensity of pure divine light. Similarly, the biblical tradition records God telling Moses, "No one can see My Face and live" (Exod. 33:20).

Nevertheless, the mystics have helped us by articulating some of the dimensions of this concealment. Probably a true map of the revelation of divine energies, if one could be drawn, would be as complicated as the descriptions of DNA structures used in biology.[6] But it is not necessary to be able to know all the intricacies to benefit from the perspective of Kabbalah, just as one need not understand physics to benefit from electricity.

Our simple model of ten basic *sefirot* is drawn in the general shape of a human body, for the body is one of the veils that these divine qualities wear. On this model, the level closest to the Divine is at the top, portrayed above the head (like the crown chakra described in the teachings of yoga). The level that manifests in the physical world is represented as at the feet. Usually this model also organizes the ten *sefirot* into three triangles. The diagram below shows the traditional connections among the *sefirot,* with the triangular relationships highlighted in bold. You will see this diagram, and segments of it, frequently throughout the book. You can also imagine it as a tree with its roots in heaven, and the flowers and fruit arrayed along the branches below.

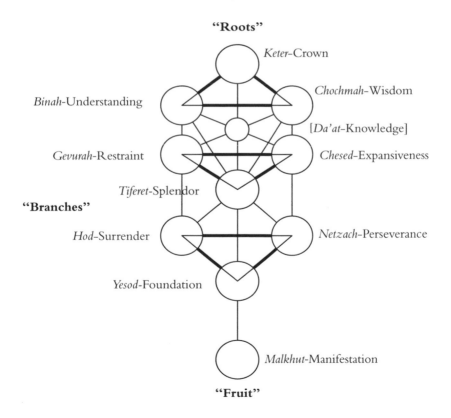

"Roots"

Keter-Crown

Chochmah-Wisdom

Binah-Understanding

[*Da'at*-Knowledge]

Gevurah-Restraint

Chesed-Expansiveness

Tiferet-Splendor

"Branches"

Hod-Surrender

Netzach-Perseverance

Yesod-Foundation

Malkhut-Manifestation

"Fruit"

We will discuss the entire map from two different perspectives. The first perspective, in Part II, is from the top down: how the divine energies transform and manifest themselves proceeding from God's emanation of divine light to the world as we know it. I am calling this perspective the "Unfolding of Creation." In Part III, I will describe the *sefirot* as also the "Path of Remembering." This approach will view the *sefirot* as a multiplicity of voices. This mode of understanding will take us on a more circuitous route, beginning at the bottom of the diagram and moving up the tree in terms of stages of development, but also spiraling through the *sefirot* to indicate their interrelationships. Ultimately, this process will bring us into the depths of our hearts, where we unify our human selves with the Divine. Moving along the paths of the Tree in both these ways will make it easier to understand how the *sefirot* apply to different areas of life.

Now it is time to add the names of the *sefirot*. You will probably want to memorize and review them often, as they are part of the basic vocabulary of Kabbalah. Then we will go to the beginning—the head—to start our course through the divine creative process.

THE TEN SEFIROT

HEBREW	ENGLISH	POSITION ON BODY	MEANING
Keter	Crown	crown of head	divine spark; will; soul
Chochmah	Wisdom	right temple	first emanation of light; spark of inspiration; seed of thought

THE TEN SEFIROT *(continued)*

HEBREW	ENGLISH	POSITION ON BODY	MEANING
Binah	Understanding	left temple	nourishing the spark into a flame, the seed into an organism
[Da'at*]	Knowledge	brain stem and spinal cord	"eleventh *sefirah*"— unifying and connecting knowledge
Chesed	Expansiveness	right shoulder and arm	lovingkindness; divine grace and universal support
Gevurah	Restraint	left shoulder and arm	discipline; limitation; strength of character
Tiferet	Splendor	heart and solar plexus	harmonic balance of tendencies; the "bolt" that unites and binds all the *sefirot*
Netzach	Perseverance	right hip and leg	energetic initiative; stamina
Hod	Surrender	left hip and leg	acceptance; yielding
Yesod	Foundation	womb and genitals	processing and transmitting energies of the preceding *sefirot*
Malkhut	Manifestation	feet and lips (as organ of speech to outside world)	"Kingship," *Shekhinah;* the final impression made on the physical world; divine presence immanent in the world

★Da'at is included in many kabbalistic schemas as an alternate to *Keter,* because *Keter* is regarded as beyond description. See pp. 47–49.

PART II

THE UNFOLDING OF CREATION

3

DIVINE MIND

With wisdom God founded the earth,
with understanding God established the heavens
and with God's knowledge the depths are broken up.
—PROVERBS 3:19–20

THE DIVINE SEA OF CONSCIOUSNESS

KABBALAH TEACHES THAT THE UNIVERSE begins with a thought
of God—or rather, an arising of will, something that comes
even before a thought. We might imagine this as a flicker of
desire that arose in the infinite allness-nothingness, what the
Jewish mystics call *Ein Sof*, "There Is No End." Scientists have
described the beginning as a wave or ripple in an infinite sea
of energy, intensifying to become that unimaginably hot point
from which the universe was born. That first ripple was will,
the desire to create. It is called *Keter*-Crown.

Every time that will rippled through the emerging cosmos, each wave was a new occurrence of potential, which is
called *Chochmah*-Wisdom. As waves interacted and created res-
onances with each other, patterns emerged. These patterns are
known as *Binah*-Understanding. We call all these occurrences
"God's thoughts." But, according to the Bible, "'My thoughts
are not your thoughts,' says God" (Isa. 55:8). The form that the

infinite light takes is not that of ordinary mental operations such as reasoning and calculating. The mind of God—God's will and wisdom, as the mystics often refer to it, similar to the Logos of Christian theology—is the power behind each new burst of creativity in the universe. Our human words, such as *will, thought,* and *mind,* are far too small for us to imagine the entity behind the creation of an entire universe, let alone many universes as Kabbalah suggests.

The levels we are trying to describe are represented in the system of Kabbalah as *sefirot* of the head. The three aspects of universal mind are portrayed in traditional kabbalistic diagrams as *sefirot* at the crown and the right and left temples. The crown is physically the fontanel, the opening in a newborn baby's skull where the bones have not completely grown together. We come to earth still open to our heavenly connection. The right and left temples hint at the other two *sefirot* of the head, Wisdom and Understanding. A fourth quasi-*sefirah* of the head known as *Da'at*-Knowledge also appears in medieval and later mysticism.

Kabbalah reminds us that these three (or four) energies are so intimately interrelated that they are really one. Christians interested in Kabbalah sometimes claimed that the triad of "first-level" divine emanations referred to the Trinity, the concept of God as three-in-one. There is no evidence, however, that Christian ideas of the Trinity influenced the triadic structure; rather, the quote from Proverbs at the head of this chapter gives the root textual source. The Neoplatonic idea of various "emanations" from the one probably had some impact on both traditions, but each developed its own distinctive interpretations.

Moreover, the mystics emphasized that nothing about the variety of divine attributes or manifestations should ever be

conceived as undermining God's unity. The greatest affirmation in Judaism is the statement, *Shema Yisrael Adonai Elohenu,
Adonai Echad*—Hear, O Israel! The Lord is our God, the Lord
is One! Rabbi Abraham Isaac Kook, chief rabbi of Palestine
from 1920 until his death in 1935, wrote that this sentence
contains the most powerful thought a person can think. If we
want to relate to the mind of God, our first act must be to
affirm God's unity—that God is one and the only one, the
source of all unity:

> The affirmation of the unity of God aspires to reveal the
> unity in the world, in man, among nations, and in the
> entire content of existence.... This is the most august
> thought among the great thoughts that man's intellectual
> capacity can conceive. It is revealed to him through his
> receptivity to spiritual illumination. It may take him to
> the height of a revelation of the Divine, by the way of rea-
> son, the knowledge called "face to face."[1]

Our yearnings toward universality, our intuition that we are all
one, our knowledge that God is one—all are messages
engraved within us by the original mind. As the famous physicist David Bohm wrote, "The universe is one seamless, unbroken whole."[2]

The term for head in Hebrew has the same root as the
term for beginning. These *sefirot* of the head connect to and
undergird all creative developments in the entire universe,
reaching down to all conscious mental activity on this planet.
But, like the submerged portion of an iceberg, their activity
is beyond our conscious awareness. The activity of the mind
of God is not unconscious in the sense of a lower-level, physical activity, but rather "transconscious," going beyond the

awareness of our normal waking state. These *sefirot* of the head are called "the hidden things" because they are completely invisible until they express themselves at a more accessible level. As we try to explicate and make them "visible" in the next few sections, remember that we are always straining to express the inexpressible, using the best metaphors we can find.

THE BEGINNINGS OF DESIRE: *KETER*-CROWN

The highest *sefirah* on the Tree of Life is known as *Keter*-Crown, or will. The Hebrew term for will also means desire. The first thing that had to happen for a universe to appear is that it had to be willed; or, a desire arose. In retrospect, we say that God wanted to create a world. But already the words define what was as yet undefined—most simply, a will that resulted in some change from what was. Will is the origin of creativity.

The metaphor of crown tells us something else about will. We find that not only in Judaism but also in Hinduism's yogic tradition the highest energy point of a person is called the crown—the crown chakra. A crown is a physical metaphor or symbol for a higher energy that, for people who can perceive it, hovers above the head. In medieval paintings it was represented as a halo. Kings, priests, and other officials were supposed to have access to this crown energy and perhaps began wearing gold diadems studded with jewels to make sure that their subjects recognized that their authority derived from a higher power—whether they deserved it or not! On a spiritual level, the energy above the head is a kind of light that emanates from the soul.

The most advanced theories in biology suggest that some conceptual construct, similar to the idea of a crown, is necessary to explain the amazing capacity of organisms to grow in a certain direction and regenerate themselves. The Jewish mystics say that everything, even a blade of grass, has an angel that says to it, "Grow! Grow!" Similarly, we often speak of the will to live as a powerful force in life. In Kabbalah, this power of will is an energy that points to a goal.

Crown is expressed in a particular name of God found in the Bible, the name revealed to Moses at the burning bush: *Ehyeh asher Ehyeh,* "I will be what I will be." This means that because everything is the unfolding of the divine will to be, all of creation is connected to God's ultimate oneness. Biologically, the human species came from one genetic source; on a spiritual level, humanity also has only one source. In Kabbalah, this is referred to as the primordial Adam (*adam* means "human being," generically). This Adam was, as we saw earlier, made precisely "in the image of God." Ancient sources portray primordial Adam as a gigantic personage shining with light who could see from one end of the world to the other. Every human being that exists or has ever existed is connected to that original Adam; collectively we are that Adam. On the personal level, Judaism teaches that the soul is completely pure because of its connection to the divine essence represented in the Crown. No matter what happens while the soul is in a physical incarnation on earth, nothing can harm the soul or disrupt its inherent connection to God. Moreover, our soul is always trying to express its true essence through our lives.

Because we are given free choice, we have the possibility of tuning out our soul connection, so to speak. Over time, blockages can develop, a kind of hardening of the spiritual arteries, in the mental, emotional, and physical channels through which the soul is trying to express itself. But the soul remains—disappointed perhaps, in not being able to do its work completely, but without changing its unique essence. This means that it is always possible for a person to return to the source, to return to God, for there is an ultimate divine anchor in the soul of each one of us. This absolute ability to return—in Hebrew *teshuvah*—is built into the structure of the universe itself. This is one of the meanings of ultimate oneness.

WISDOM AND WILDNESS: *CHOCHMAH*-WISDOM

Energy from the Crown emanates forth a "supernal luminescence" that is called *Chochmah*-Wisdom. It is an experiment, an exploration, the emergence of the possibility of "something" even though it is "nothing" yet. This *sefirah* is the channel for creative force in the entire cosmos. In the natural world, the result is amazing and totally unpredictable diversity. In the human world, the results are inspiration and revelation, including what is called illumination in mysticism. Experiences of Wisdom are the foundation of all the world's religious traditions and the origin of multitudes of great creative endeavors.

On the cosmic level, we know now that the universe cannot be accidental, the result of random collisions of atoms. There has to be some source of form or organization—what we would colloquially call purpose—in the universe as we know it. If the universe is in some sense "aimed at," Wisdom is the bow that shoots the arrow toward the target. We cannot see this bow, just as we cannot see the elementary particles hypothesized by physicists. But just as scientists track the movements of particles with sophisticated instruments and find their imprints scattered on a screen, so we infer the *sefirah* of Wisdom from its results—creativity and diversity.

The mystics turned to a passage from the biblical Book of Proverbs to extol Wisdom's role in creation, in a metaphorical way that expresses the joy of this divine energy:

> The Lord created me [Wisdom] the beginning of his
>   works,
> Before all else that he made, long ago ...
> When there was yet no ocean I was born, ...
> When he set the heavens in their place I was there ...
> And knit together earth's foundations.
> Then I was at his side each day, his darling and delight,
> Playing in his presence continually,
> Playing on the earth, when he had finished it,
> While my delight was in humankind. (Prov. 8:22–31)

This kind of wisdom is not expressed directly in words—what could express the "playing" of God? We can take a hint from mathematical cosmologist Brian Swimme's description of the wildness in natural evolution. Speaking of the conscious choice of animals as they moved into new territory, he writes:

> Their movement into their future evolution began with commitment to a vision—a vision strongly felt but seen as if fleetingly and in darkness. Perhaps it was just the sheer thrill of the gallop that captivated the first horse's consciousness and convinced it to make that species-determining decision: "We will run, come what may." No vision of itself in the future, and yet the future pressed into its experience of the moment: "Here is a way to live. Here is a path worth risking everything for."[3]

The divine Wisdom, and all our fleeting glimpses of it, comes from a place beyond stasis and stability, engendering an act "worth risking everything for." With such an act, God created the universe.

Wisdom is often referred to as being like a flash of lightning, probably because of its extraordinary brilliance and ability to illuminate everything simultaneously. The phrase "flash of inspiration" carries some of the same meaning. Lightning is one of the experiences recorded of the ancient Israelites at Mount Sinai, the core revelation of Judaism. The accounts of that experience suggest profound levels of transformation—for example, the Torah comments that they "saw the voices." This statement hints at a much larger experience than simply hearing words spoken, as Rabbi Schneur Zalman of Liadi, founder of the Chabad school of Hasidism, explains:

> "It was *shown*," actually with physical vision, as it is written, "And all the people saw the voices" (Exod. 20:15)— "they *saw* what is [normally] heard." And the Rabbis of blessed memory explained, "They looked eastward and heard the speech issuing forth, 'I am,' etc., and so toward the four points of the compass, and upward and downward," as is explained ... that "There was no place from which God did not speak to them...." Therefore the Israelites repeatedly fainted out of existence, as the Rabbis taught, "At each utterance their soul took flight, ... but the Blessed-Holy-One restored it to them with the dew with which He will revive the dead."[4]

These descriptions allude to time/space dissolution, synesthesia (crossover of types of sensory perception), and altered states of consciousness. Similar experiences of illumination and insight in many mystical traditions are unusually intense in their clarity and bodily effects and potentially transformative in their results.

Kabbalists say that the *sefirah* of Wisdom manifests in the first word of the Ten Commandments: "I Am." Absolute Oneness expresses itself as "I," what we usually call a personal deity, that is, the Divine expressing itself in the metaphor of "person." Divinity that was beyond all categories willingly enters a category that we can understand, an entity that wills and acts: "I am the Lord your God who took you out of Egypt." This is the most concrete expression of the act worth risking everything for—to choose human beings to join God in creating a better world.

The creative powers of this *sefirah* include the creation of the roots of entities called souls.[5] Just as one root of a plant can diversify above the surface of the ground into many stems, so there are soul roots in Wisdom that later diversify into many individual souls. Thus renowned American teacher of Kabbalah Rabbi Aryeh Kaplan comments on the famous rabbinic saying, "Who is wise? He who learns from every man" (*Avot* 4.1): "It is on the level of Wisdom that all men are one."[6] Significantly, this idea broadens our concept of soul. A soul is not limited to being a personal essence, but also, on a deeper and more hidden level, is connected to other souls across time and space. Like stars and constellations and galaxies, some souls seem to be closer than others, forming systems or clusters. Their original light is Crown; the different frequencies beginning to emerge come from Wisdom.

Whether we are aware of it or not, Wisdom means that each of us is an audacious experiment of God. Like the first shoot that ever sprouted from the earth, like the first horse about to gallop, we are each a new creation. Moreover, this creation continues. As Rabbi Abraham Isaac Kook wrote of the human spirit, "Waves from the higher realm act on our souls ceaselessly. The stirrings of our inner spiritual sensibilities are the result of the sounds released by the violin of our souls, as it listens to the echo of the sound emanating from the Divine realm."[7]

The next step in the unfolding is that the streams of light and ripples of sound from Wisdom embed themselves in the sea of consciousness called Understanding.

PATTERN AND IMAGINATION:
BINAH-UNDERSTANDING

If *Chochmah*-Wisdom is waves of energy, *Binah*-Understanding is form. At the level of divinity, God "under-stands" and upholds the forms that creation can take. From the perspective of our world, Understanding, like Wisdom, is still only potential—indeed, Rabbi Nachman of Breslov called this *sefirah* the "world to come." This means that it contains divine light and supreme knowledge, which cannot be revealed completely now, but only in a future state.[8] Still, Understanding has more structure and is closer to our world than the flashes of Wisdom. Symbolically, Understanding represents the mother-matrix; in more modern terms, she is the divine template or pattern of existence.

The description of Understanding as mother and Wisdom as father comes from ancient teachings and is very prominent in the *Zohar*. We must recognize that at the level of the upper *sefirot* there is really no gender, for all such distinctions belong to the lower world of duality. But as metaphors, "father" and "mother" express a fundamental aspect of the creative process in terms that we can immediately grasp. Father brings forth a seed, which cannot grow on its own; it needs the nourishment of the mother's womb. "The *potentia* of the world (the seed of *Chochmah*) is externalized and individuated in the womb of *Binah* but remains concealed like a foetus. Therefore *Binah* is called the concealed world."[9]

Binah-Understanding as "womb" is reminiscent of the Great Mother of archetypal mythology and psychology, the matrix out of which differences and relationships are born. It may have been an inner awareness of the aspect of divine mother that led ancient and medieval Christians to elevate Mary, mother of Jesus, to a higher-than-human status. The kabbalists described *Binah* as the "vacated space," the hollow carved out of Infinity so that a finite universe could exist.[10] In that sense, Understanding represents the beginning of separation, the world created through divine contraction. Still, at her level differences do not create opposition but only harmony. As the mystics put it, "Lovingkindness alone manifests" in the upper three *sefirot,* and, quoting the Book of Psalms, "The world is built [the Hebrew word for build is related to *binah*] on lovingkindness" (Ps. 89:3). *Binah*-Understanding is like a sea of divine consciousness in which our personal minds swim.

Because the upper *sefirot* are deeply united, the triangle shape in which the first three *sefirot* are traditionally represented may be somewhat misleading. It suggests that the father and mother are dualistic opposites, set across from one another as the base of a triangle. We can also see their relationships in the following form, recalling a seed in the womb:

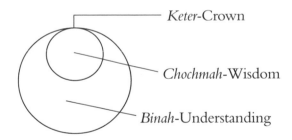

Keter-Crown

Chochmah-Wisdom

Binah-Understanding

Another approach is suggested by the way the kabbalists placed these three energies in the human body. Crown is at the fontanel, Wisdom is in the space between the skull and the membrane of the brain, and Understanding is connected to both the center of the brain and to the right side of the heart.

How does Understanding operate? As divine/soul energy moves from Wisdom to Understanding, it enters into the mother–matrix. While this is still a hidden world, it nevertheless gives a certain level of formation and expression to the abstract vibrations of Wisdom. Some force draws sparks of energy toward one another so that they bond and become what we might be able to recognize as thoughts, or even more fundamentally, images or metaphors. Like gravity in the physical cosmos, Understanding makes it possible for ideas and patterns to have stability.

Understanding may be related to what some mystics have called the "third eye" (Hinduism's sixth chakra). Telepathic events, dreams, and prophecies emerge from this overarching consciousness. Understanding represents information—information—that belongs to anyone. My young daughter once told me, quoting the elderly rabbi who was her first-grade teacher, "When you have an idea, remember that it is just part of what's floating around out there, and you happened to be the one to pluck it out of the air." This also helps explain why significant discoveries in science often occur almost simultaneously in two or more different laboratories.

Commonly, information coming from Understanding encodes itself in images, as in dreams. Understanding is also connected to the heart and to feelings of deep joy because "the meditation of my heart will be understanding" (Ps. 49:3). This multileveled characteristic of Understanding, its heart-mind connection, suggests that it pervades many aspects of our unconscious as well as our conscious selves.

Most fundamentally, it provides the templates to which all the other *sefirot* relate. As I indicated when discussing Wisdom, religions are usually rooted in fundamental revelations from some spiritual source that provides a unique way of accessing higher realms. The "flash" or seed of the revelation is Wisdom, and its elaboration into a basic pattern is Understanding. In Judaism, with the revelation known as the giving of the Torah, we saw that the experience of Wisdom is embedded in the word "I Am." The form-creating qualities of Understanding are represented in the Ten Commandments—ten principles that fleshed out the Wisdom and became a template for all of Jewish life for millennia to come. In other ways, the revelation of the Qur'an in Islam, the enlightenment of the Buddha, and Jesus's resurrection in Christianity formed a basic pattern for each religion.

To say this *sefirah* provides for the formation of a template or matrix means that it yields a pattern that can be filled with different contents. In other words, Understanding tells us that, prior to our ordinary thinking, there exists a pattern that governs our thinking. Every society imprints its unconscious patterns on its members through language and customary behavior. Every religious and spiritual tradition seeks to imprint a different and higher template than society's, urging us to live on another level. I spoke of the will of the soul, coming from *Keter*-Crown, as an angel that says to the blade of grass, "Grow!" Here, on a more concrete level, the template of a tradition is like an angelic model that offers a focus for aspiration: "Grow toward this ideal!"

The idea of a template is configured physically in a temple. Architecturally, a physical temple creates a sacred space that conveys the underlying patterns of a tradition. The original temple of Judaism was a portable sanctuary or tabernacle that incorporated cosmic symbolism in its components and structures.[11] In a parallel fashion, the medieval cathedral, with its cruciform shape, its great sculptures and stained glass, told the stories that informed European Christianity's basic template. The method by which Understanding enters human consciousness is what we call "contemplation"—literally, contemplate-ing, integrating the template into yourself. Most traditions have some form of contemplative meditation, prayer, or repetitive practice that helps a disciple internalize the template of the tradition. Psalms or hymns, chants or dances entrain images and metaphors with rhythm and melody to help practitioners integrate the basic elements of faith.

Judaism has several interrelated templates, all expressing the will of God *(Keter)*. First is the Ten Commandments, whose words brought God's will down to earth in discursive form. The remainder of the Torah, including Judaism's "Oral Torah" (discussions of laws, at first transmitted orally but later written down), amplifies and clarifies the ten basic principles. Another template is the image of the desert sanctuary that was revealed to Moses in a vision. It expressed the divine will to manifest on earth, as "God's house." Being in God's house became an important metaphor for connection to God: "Happy are those who sit in Your house!" (Ps. 145); "Only one thing I seek: to stay in the House of the Lord all the days of my life" (Ps. 27). "Let them make me a sanctuary, that I may dwell among them" (Exod. 25:8) became a guiding image for transforming the world. Yet another version of the template is the Tree of Life that emerged in kabbalistic thought, exactly what we are studying in this book. This template helps us grasp in a personal way, in our own bodies and selves, the fundamental understanding that God wants to be manifest in this world: *Keter*-Crown seeks to evolve into *Malkhut*-Manifestation.

All these images involve mind, imagination, and heart engaged with the basic template, which is intended to be internalized in each individual's body, mind, and soul. You may want to think about the templates that have informed Christianity as you know it, historically and contemporaneously. For example, Christians have often meditated on the sufferings of Jesus and recounted the stories of his goodness. Such reflection is not merely an esoteric exercise. The point of all such practices is to remake the mind—and ultimately the body—as the "temple of the soul," meaning, in the image of the religious ideal.

This work is very important because, from the perspective of Kabbalah, *the entire organism suffers when it has no deeper template.* We also suffer if the template we are taught to internalize is out of alignment with the truth of life as we encounter it (which, as we will see, is the work of the lower *sefirot*). Thus the *sefirah* of Understanding is one of the keys to our crucial task as human beings: to restore wholeness to life. In fact, the study of Kabbalah itself is one of Understanding's methods because it asks us to reflect on the basic template of creation. The fragments we learn in any intellectual or practical endeavor can ultimately be enfolded in a unified understanding by relating them to the basic template of Understanding. As Rabbi Mordecai Miller, one of the great ethical writers in modern Judaism, explains, "Only through contemplation, the concentrated tracing of experience back through effect and cause to the first Cause of all, can man attain wholeness and unity within himself."[12]

UNIFICATION AND INTELLECT: *DA'AT*-KNOWLEDGE

Wholeness and unity—how do we achieve that? On the one hand, it must be a gift, since it comes from a world beyond human reality. Yet, as with everything in the higher worlds, we have reflections of unity within ourselves. These reflections appear as the *sefirot* that stand on the central column of the Tree, at the levels of intellect, character attributes, and action. Here we will consider a quality called *Da'at*-Knowledge, an eleventh *sefirah* emphasized by many mystics since the time of the *Zohar. Da'at*-Knowledge is actually not an independent energy of its own but is formed by the confluence of Wisdom and Understanding and is also regarded as the externalization of the hidden Crown. The term *da'at* appears early in the Bible, for the forbidden tree is called the Tree of *Da'at,* or knowledge of good and evil. Also, when the Torah speaks of the union of Adam and Eve, it uses the same term—Adam "knew" his wife. This tells us that the energy that is called "knowledge" has a particular role in the human world, an intimate or internalized knowledge.

Thus while Crown is beyond human comprehension, Knowledge is oneness, unification, in the mirror of human intellect. It is what we might call the process of integration. When we study a subject so thoroughly that we internalize it, so that something we learn becomes second nature, we have a sense of unity with that knowledge. An artist who studies the great masters and then incorporates what she has learned in her own paintings is using Knowledge. Their inspiration and their kinds of artistic vision become hers, so that Knowledge is receiving from Wisdom and Understanding and transmitting them to the lower *sefirot.* Knowledge is represented in the body by the brain stem and spinal cord, which are the messengers of neural impulses from the brain throughout the rest of the body.[13]

Knowledge implies "the limitation and finiteness of a knower, a known, and a knowing."[14] Yet despite the finitude of a human being, kabbalists hold that we can glimpse oneness through our minds. Rational intelligence, artistic awareness, and meditative contemplation are methods that have been used in all religions. We will discuss some of these methods further in a later section on basic spiritual practices. Knowledge is the mental work we do when it serves our higher desire to seek unity rather than our lower urges to satisfy egotistical needs. This *sefirah* is the human intellectual and contemplative reflection of Crown. While its manifestations are diverse, its aim is one.

Now we must shift our attention. We have gazed toward the higher *sefirot* and glimpsed a realm of open, free creativity, with the emergence of profound and magical forms. These forms speak to us from levels beyond our ordinary existence, of a world of majesty and glory, of the source of all that is. Moving from this higher level to the reality in which we normally live and breathe—the everyday world rather than the sacred space of prayer and contemplation—is a leap across a great divide. Metaphorically, it means crossing the firmament between the upper worlds and the lower worlds (Gen. 1:7).

A *midrash* says that when God created the firmament to split the lower from the upper waters, the lower waters complained. God comforted them, saying, "You will be the source of salt, and no offering will be made on My altar without salt." The salty oceans are, of course, the source of life as we know it. Life in the lower worlds is an offering on the altar, a service to God.

4

DIVINE ENERGIES

Man is composed of all the spiritual entities, and he is
perfect in all attributes, and he was created with great
wisdom ... for he comprises all the secrets of the Chariot
and his soul is linked therein, even though man is in this
world. Know that, unless man would be perfect in all the
forces of the Blessed-Holy-One, he would be unable to
do as he does.... There is a great supernal power in men,
which cannot be described.

—*SEFER HA-NE'ELAM*

A WORLD OF MULTIPLICITY

IN THE BIBLICAL CREATION STORY, there is a moment when the
upper and lower waters are separated by a great expanse usually called in English a firmament. We can imagine the firmament as that thin line—not really a physical line—between the
ocean and the sky on a clear day. On the upper side of the line
is *Binah*-Understanding, leading to heavenly levels of consciousness. *Da'at*-Knowledge sits immediately below the line,
connecting to the world of finite human experience. The
regions further beneath the line are worlds of separation:
instead of oneness, multiplicity.

Yet they are also worlds of dynamism—flowing, surging, holding back—a world of almost constant movement. Here, it is as if God were saying, "I have created opposites, upper and lower, black and white, left and right. Now bring them together. Live in the lower world from the higher perspective of the world of unity."

On the Tree of Life, the world of multiplicity is represented by the seven lower *sefirot*. The *sefirot* of the left and right sides represent opposites, while those of the center are unifying forces, each with its own distinctive quality.

The first six of these seven lower *sefirot* compose a pattern of dynamic energy, which comes to rest at the last *sefirah* of *Malkhut*-Manifestation. The six *sefirot* are also called the *midot,* which literally means "measures." This hints to the fact that, unlike the first three *sefirot* of the head, which are essentially one or unmeasured, these principles have limits—indeed, as we will see, they limit one another. Like the measurements of an architect in designing the form of a building, they create the frame of life. They also create the frame of the human body. While the first three *sefirot* are those of the head, the next six are frequently portrayed as two triads, represented on the body as the upper and lower torso—the heart and abdominal cavities. The last *sefirah* is at the feet.

The word *midot* also means attributes. They are qualities that can be discerned in the world, something like character traits in a person. They are qualities of God-in-the-world, and qualities we can see in people. We will discuss personal aspects of all the attributes in Part III. Here we will focus on their larger significance.

We will begin with the two uppermost *sefirot, Chesed*-Expansiveness and *Gevurah*-Restraint, which constitute the basic expression of duality in the universe.

DYNAMICS OF DUALITY

If you have read books on Kabbalah before, you have probably seen these two *sefirot* called by other names—Lovingkindness and Strength, Love and Power, Compassion and Discipline. I use a more impersonal terminology, Expansiveness and Restraint, to emphasize that these *sefirot* do not represent merely human qualities, but are basic to the entire universe as we know it. The reason we can easily find parallels to them in the details of our emotions and relationships is that these qualities can be found in everything. Indeed, they are sometimes used to describe the two sides of the entire Tree of Life.

Chesed-Expansiveness and *Gevurah*-Restraint are the foundation of the known universe because they are principles of duality, opposites, counterforces. Their primal dynamic is captured in the following description of the conditions of the universe's emerging:

> In the primeval fireball, which quickly billowed in every direction, we see a metaphor for the infinite striving of the sentient being. An unbridled playing out of this cosmic tendency would lead to ultimate dispersion. But the fireball discovered a basic obstacle to its movements, the gravitational attraction. Only because expansion met the obstacle of gravitation did the galaxies come forth.... Many of the inventions of the natural world arose out of beings meeting the constraints of the universe with creative response. Only by dealing with the difficulty does the creativity come forth.... The beauty of the response arises from an inherently difficult situation.[1]

The billowing out of the fireball is an expression of Expansiveness, while the obstacle of gravitational attraction, a fundamental constraint of the universe, is Restraint. The diffi-culty leads to beauty, which happens to be one of the names of the central *sefirah* at the heart, *Tiferet*-Splendor.

Everywhere we encounter fundamental dualities: light and darkness, movement and rest, male and female, fire and water, positive and negative poles of electromagnetism. "Twoness" is also the dynamic of creator and creation. In this sense, Expansiveness and Restraint are intimately involved in the creation of the universe. When God only was present— when Divinity was totally expanded, we might say—no world was possible. The famous kabbalist Rabbi Isaac Luria, known as The Ari, explained that God contracted himself, bringing into being a hollow space, which we saw was compared to *Binah,* inside the fullness. This was an act of Restraint. Into this space, God emanated a beam of light, known as the *Or Ein Sof,* or light of the infinite. From this all creation emerged— Expansiveness again.

Through that divine self-restraint, another reality was made possible, a universe unfolding in the vacated space, a world that appears to be sustained by its own laws.[2] After the first expansion of the universe, its elements cooled—they were "restrained," and stars could form. The forces of Expansiveness and Restraint are elegantly presented in the picture of the solar system, where planets circle the sun at massive speeds, with enough energy to hurl themselves out into the universe, except that the bond of gravity or restraint keeps turning them slightly toward the sun, creating ellipses as their trail.

Religions have been based on the dual principle—for example, the battle of light with darkness, or God versus Satan. Yin and yang are opposites understood as fundamental to the universe in the traditional Chinese worldview. Our biblical cre-ation story distinguishes upper from lower waters, water from dry land, vegetation from animals, and so on. Spirit energizes the waters *(Expansiveness)*. The waters are gathered *(Restraint)* so that dry land can appear. The earth produces growth *(Expansiveness)*, and each produces seed "according to its kind" *(Restraint)*.

Making distinctions and recognizing opposites is also a basic human task. One of the blessings in the Jewish prayer book, said daily in the morning, thanks God for our power to make distinctions: "Blessed are You, Lord our God, Ruler of the Universe, who gives the mind the power to distinguish day from night." Making distinctions is not a bad thing; neither are what we call opposites. Judaism also has a blessing specifically for appreciating distinctions, a blessing recited at the end of Shabbat on Saturday night:

> Blessed are You, Lord our God, Ruler of the Universe, Who distinguishes between the sacred and the profane, between light and darkness, between Israel and the peoples, between the seventh day and the six days of creation. Blessed are You, Lord, Who distinguishes between the holy and the ordinary.

Indeed, making appropriate distinctions is one of the ways that the original mistake of Adam and Eve can be corrected. The forbidden tree was the Tree of Knowledge of Good and Evil. When they ate of the fruit, good and evil became mixed and confused in the world. The human task is to clarify the difference between them and choose the good.

LOVE AND LIMITATION

Chesed-Expansiveness creates the possibility of existence as we know it. That is why it is traditionally called Lovingkindness. It is the force of giving and going-out-toward, an energy that wants an "other" to exist and flourish. Expansiveness is the root

55

of the concept of a loving Creator, which is deeply embedded in Western religions. The source of the universe has the desire to bestow existence, goodness, and blessing on another entity. The rabbinic tradition says that God's mercy sustains the universe—if it were not so, the world would not stand.[3]

On the human level, the Torah's essential message is lovingkindness. In many Jewish prayers, and in Islam as well, God is called "the Compassionate One." In Christianity, the expansiveness of divine love has been a part of its theology since its earliest beginnings: "God so loved the world"; "Love never ends" (John 3:16; 1 Cor. 13:8). While Eastern religions do not focus so much on the personality of a deity, still we see the attribute of outgoing love in the Buddha, who is sometimes called "the Heart of Compassion," and the Bodhisattvas, who wish to free all beings from enslavement to desire.

The other side of the duality is *Gevurah*-Restraint. This *sefirah* embodies the possibility that something independent can exist, something that is not entirely dependent on its creator. If God had never contracted, there would be no universe. Out of God's restraint, the universe can evolve. With gravity, the universe can attain stability. On the human level, restraint is justice. The desires of individual beings are restrained by laws and courts on behalf of the larger community, which would otherwise dissipate into chaos.

Understand that Restraint is the opposite of Expansiveness—but also that these two *sefirot* are opposite poles of one whole. Both come from the wholeness of love. Love as Expansiveness expresses itself in total support of being, saying yes! to every movement of freedom and self-expression. Love identifies with growth, well-being, and happiness and puts itself behind entities acting for the good. Parental love is a good example—think of a parent who takes the hands of an infant who is struggling to stand, helping the child find his balance. On the other hand, Restraint is also an act of love. If we really love others, we know that we cannot overwhelm them with our support, in effect doing everything for them. Thus the parent will also sometimes exercise restraint, standing back and letting the child struggle to stand on his own and develop independence.

Once specific identities emerge, the conditions of life change. In a universe of entities that have different identities—the world of not only duality but also multiplicity—every time one entity expresses Expansiveness, others will of necessity have to experience Restraint. Your self-expression is a boundary to mine, and mine a boundary to yours. Out of mutual respect, we allow this to be the case—I restrain myself from invading your boundaries, and you do the same. We wish that such balance and respect would operate harmoniously, out of the love that embraces all beings. Such a world would be like living among the angels—as the Jewish liturgy says, each company of angels gives permission to the other to take its turn at praising God. No pushing and shoving in heaven!

Here, it doesn't work that way. This brings us to the second important aspect of the duality of Expansiveness and Restraint: On a practical level, it is impossible to have a world of different, unique, individual entities where suffering does not occur. When a volcano expresses Expansiveness, the heat and force that produce molten lava can cause severe limitations to the plants, animals, and human beings around it. From an objective viewpoint, nature is simply taking its course. But if we take account of the experience of the beings affected, we must recognize that they experience pain. At the moment the molten lava imposes restrictions, the animals must experience loss of support and a blockade of the fulfillment of their potential. These experiences are possible outcomes of limitation, of Restraint.

From the interactive, interinclusive duality of Expansiveness and Restraint—loving support and independence—arises a universe of interdependent beings, including the whole range from subatomic particles to human beings, angelic forces, and God. Because God chose to create in this way, God, too, is interdependent with us. This fact lies behind a mysterious statement in the *Zohar*, that the "arousal from above" depends on the "arousal from below." The arousal from above is God's action; the arousal from below is human action. God depends on us, and we on God. Abraham Heschel, drawing on Hasidic tradition, stated it explicitly: "God is in need of man." We are in need of one another, and of plants, animals, and minerals. Reciprocity is built into the structure of the universe. Expansiveness and Restraint are the poles of that reciprocity.

Moreover, Restraint has traditionally been referred to as punishment or judgment. To borrow a metaphor from galactic experience, it is like the consuming fire of a star dying, becoming a black hole, pulling all matter into its intense gravitational field. On the human level, the effect can range from confusion to overwhelming loneliness to fear of death. The kabbalists called it the experience of chaos and dread. As the ancient text known as the *Bahir* says about the attribute of Restraint:

> It is Chaos. It emanates from evil and astounds people. And what is that? It is that regarding which it is written, "And fire came down and it consumed the burnt offering, and the stones, and the earth, and it evaporated the water that was in the trench" (1 Kings 18:38). It is also written, "The Lord your God is a consuming fire, a jealous God" (Deut. 4:24).[4]

When God expresses Restraint, some of the ordering force of the universe is removed, and that is why it is experienced as chaos.

Some theologians have spoken of Restraint as the absence of God. Yet, as the Hasidic masters teach, we cannot say God is absent from the world. If God really abandoned a relationship with the universe, everything would cease to exist. We can't even say that Restraint has to do with "bad things" happening, while Expansiveness is about "good things." Unlimited blessings can also have negative effects. Rain is a blessing for crops, but too much rain—too much Expansiveness—is not good either. (The traditional Jewish prayers for rain ask that the rain come "for a blessing and not for a curse.") The stories of people who win the lottery and then find their lives much too complicated are another example. On the other hand, what first appears to be negative may turn out to be for the good.

We tend to see the aspects of Expansiveness and Restraint through the lenses of linear time, rather than through the more comprehensive space-time of higher levels. Since we cannot see future good results that come from something we experience as evil, or the future evil from something that looks great to us, we seesaw our way through life. We hardly need to mention this in a Christian context, since Christian theology has delved deeply into the redemptive possibilities of suffering. But we can see it on both a collective and an individual level. Slavery in Egypt was the paradigmatic experience through which the Jewish people developed attributes of compassion and mercy. Grief can lead to transformation: People who lose beloved family members often take action to prevent the same happening to others. Imprisonment can be devastating, but some use the opportunity to develop inner strength. We usually don't realize that both dimensions of the duality are always present, for we can see only part of the picture at any given time. Do you recall events in your own life that you thought were disasters, but then it turned out that something better evolved from precisely that difficult situation?

Kabbalah offers us a unique perspective here. In the big picture, on the level of unification, God's sustenance of the universe is itself a tremendous act of ongoing love. This love indeed never ends, or stops even for a moment. But, on the lower level where we live, God appears to be dealing out judgment and punishment. The lower dualistic level is understood as the revealed, while the higher unified reality is the concealed. The great seventeenth-century kabbalist Rabbi Moshe Chaim Luzzato describes these levels:

> In all of God's dealings with us we can posit two dimensions, the revealed and the concealed. The revealed is reward and punishment (to the recipient of one or the other, good or bad). The concealed is the deep design inhering always in all of His deeds, to guide the creation to the universal perfection. For this is certainly the case: there is no deed, small or great, whose ultimate end is not the universal perfection, as stated by our sages, "All that is done by Heaven is for the good" (*Berachot* 60b), and by the prophet: "Your wrath will turn back and You will console me" (Isa. 12:1).[5]

From this point of view, what we call evil is a withdrawal by God into a greater concealment.

A Personal God

However, the idea of balancing good and evil does not tell the whole story. We have a long tradition in the West, beginning with the Bible, of God responding to some kinds of human actions with a sharp, punishing response, while providing reward for other actions. The ancient prophets described the punishing response as God's anger or zeal. God's "consuming fire" was a direct response to human sins. Near the end of Deuteronomy, the last book of the written Torah, this divine response is described as a hiding of the divine face. "Then My anger will be roused against them and I will abandon them and hide My face from them.... On that day I will hide my face because of all the evil they have done in turning to other gods" (Deut. 31:17, 18). Divine favor was a direct response to repentance and good deeds.

Often, people have interpreted the stories of divine punishment as if God had an angry personality. It is important to recognize that the Bible uses many anthropomorphic expressions, both physical and psychological, to illustrate how God's actions and feelings are like those of humans. Judaism has always insisted on understanding God in a personal way. It does *not* mean that every time something bad happens, God is punishing someone. Rather, we have two perspectives on God and divine action in the world: a more impersonal one, as described above in discussing the relationship between cosmic *Chesed* and cosmic *Gevurah,* and a more personal one, which the biblical stories often portray in terms of God's love and punishment. The question is, how can the two perspectives be reconciled?

The sages tell us that the Torah itself shows two different ways God manifests in our world. Two names are frequently used for God in the Bible—the four-letter name Y-H-V-H (the Tetragrammaton, often written by scholars as "Yahweh"), which cannot be pronounced but is usually replaced by *Adonai,* and the name *Elohim.* These are usually translated in English Bibles as Lord and God respectively. Lord is the personal aspect of God that intervenes in history and our lives, while God is God as manifest in nature and law, balancing everything in cosmic justice. Y-H-V-H is Expansiveness, God is Restraint.

When we address God personally, we evoke that aspect of the Divine that emanates mercy and lovingkindness. Without the personal aspect, the world would become an empty shell, a mechanical object working according to laws of nature. Our lives would be subject to an automatic kind of karma, in which the fruits of our actions would weigh heavily upon us and progress would be very difficult. Judaism has a concept similar to karma in the metaphor of the scales upon which each person's deeds are weighed every year at Rosh Hashanah (the Jewish New Year). But Judaism also insists that because of God's mercy, we can ask forgiveness and wipe the slate clean. The natural balancing of Expansiveness and Restraint might lead to an equilibrium, but the divine Creator wants more than just equilibrium. By adding an extra measure of love and mercy, God ensures that the balance will come out toward the good.

This approach has some interesting implications. If God has experiences and feelings, is it true that, as the medieval philosophers said, God never changes? (In the philosophies of the Middle Ages, inherited from the ancient Greek philosophers Plato and Aristotle, change was associated with physical form and its imperfections. God, being noncorporeal, must not change.) The biblical view seems to be that God is not an objective entity or an impervious cosmic mind; rather, God responds—God has an inner life, and we can interpret God's life in terms analogous to ours as sad, pleased, regretful, angry, and, of course, loving. God's "anger," then, is the way the Bible speaks of the human experience that we are calling Restraint, while God's "love" is the way it describes what we are calling Expansiveness. Both are God. They are two sides of one coin, just as in physics wave and particle are two forms in which light can be perceived and described.

Kabbalah encourages us to think of God's relationship to us in human terms. The terms *Father* and *Mother* for two of the *sefirot* are one example. Another is the description of God's relationship with the Jewish people as being analogous to that between husband and wife. The mystics also speak of an aspect of God—the *Shekhinah,* the feminine divine presence (*Malkhut-Manifestation*)—that is "in exile" with us, exile being the condition in which we experience separation from God. We can imagine God experiencing the sphere of human activity as a chaotic and even painful part of the universe God created.

This brings out another implication, namely, that God has built into the structure of the universe ways for us to call forth the positive and diminish the negative. Human beings have the responsibility to act in ways that enhance the side of love and support. When the Bible promises rewards for certain actions such as honoring one's parents, it is prescribing modes of behavior that evoke positive responses in divine consciousness. God will respond to us in ways similar to the way we respond to one another. When we cause pain to one another, God may respond by concealing the divine countenance, as a way of urging us to call forth God's love once again. The ancient writers understood this relationship, even if their metaphors were not the same as ours; for the ancient Jewish people and their spokesmen, the experience of God's closeness was very intense, and the experience of God's distance was in the form of plague and fire. They understood that God cries out when we are neglecting our fellow human beings and when we are neglecting our spiritual lives.

One of the great teachers of the twentieth century, Abraham Joshua Heschel, wrote in this vein about the Holocaust, and it is worth pondering his words to consider how we have objectified and distanced God:

> Through centuries His voice cried in the wilderness. How skillfully it was trapped and imprisoned in the temples! How often it was drowned or distorted! Now we

behold how it gradually withdraws, abandoning one people after another, departing from their souls, despising their wisdom. The taste for the good has all but gone from the earth. Men heap spite upon cruelty, malice upon atrocity....

"Where is God? Why didst Thou not halt the trains loaded with Jews being led to slaughter?" ... Indeed, where were we when men learned to hate in the days of starvation? When raving madmen were sowing wrath in the hearts of the unemployed? ...

Our world seems not unlike a pit of snakes. We did not sink into the pit in 1939, or even in 1933. We had descended into it generations ago, and the snakes have sent their venom into the bloodstream of humanity....

God will return to us when we shall be willing to let Him in.[6]

When we abandon our divine purpose, there are likely to be consequences. *Gevurah*-Restraint means that God is leaving room for human freedom, but if we misuse it, God becomes even more concealed, and on the level of the revealed world the results are bitter, as Heschel suggested.

Still, we must also remember that not all suffering is the result of a flawed relationship to God. Viruses have a drive to exist, even at the expense of their human hosts. Humans and their machines make mistakes. Above all, we should never suggest to other people that their pain and suffering is divine punishment. Introspectively, it may sometimes be appropriate to ask whether a misalignment with divine intent is adding to our problems. *Gevurah*-Restraint asks us to go in all humility (which does not mean self-abasement or excessive self-criticism) into a deeper relationship with God.

VISION AND HIGHER PURPOSE: *TIFERET*-SPLENDOR

All our questions about pain and suffering are themselves a hint to the next level, the *sefirah* of *Tiferet*-Splendor. Our questions arise out of our inner sense of purpose, our deep belief that things ought to make sense, and our visions of ideals that could be realized. The amazing thing about the human species is that, despite all the apparently senseless sufferings, most people still believe in a larger purpose to life. That is because we possess the energy of Splendor. We see patterns, growth, and development. The patterns are no more than a dim reflection of the glowing template of the world of unity, but they give us hope. The vessel of that hope crystallizes our organizing purpose, and human energies organize themselves around it, like filings around a magnet.

The *sefirah* of Splendor represents the emergence of conscious purpose. While purpose exists at every level of creation, it does not become fully conscious until creation arrives at the first human being. In the biblical story, dualities alternate: light and dark, water and dry land, sun and moon, plants and trees, birds of the air and fish of the sea, and finally, on the sixth day, animals and humanity. Only here does God say that creation is "in His image" (Gen. 1:27), and only here does the divine breath enter a creature (Gen. 2:3). Image means the possibility of likeness: Just as God has a purpose, now creation includes a being that can embody purpose. Breath is like spirit, a force that hovered over the waters of chaos in order to begin bringing it into form. Most of all, just as God is one, so this human being is one—not dual, not divided.

As we saw earlier, the first person, Adam, contains both male and female, and is the perfect image of God the Creator. Moreover, just as the metaphor of king is used for God, so

Adam is given "dominion" over the earth. With the emergence of Adam, purpose could be made apparent. A king can have perspective over the entire kingdom and can decree in light of this great range of perception. Humanity, God's ambassador on earth, could carry forward God's project—to reveal what God intended but heretofore concealed. As one of the Hasidic masters put it, "Man is a microcosm, a miniature universe, a complete structure."[7] Similarly, philosopher David Ray Griffin states, "The human person incorporates all levels from subatomic particles to self-conscious mind."[8] Since God put all the created powers into human beings, the human species alone could execute the divine will completely.

The idea of human dominion has become suspect in recent times because we have become more aware of how human rulership over the world has led to corruption and destruction of what once was truly a paradise. In less than two hundred years since the beginning of the Industrial Revolution, we have changed the face of a unique planet where life evolved into amazingly diverse, beautiful, and intelligent forms into one where thousands of species, and the quality of life itself, are being threatened by our chemicals and concrete. People concerned about the health of the earth have questioned whether human existence should be given the preeminent value that biblical tradition has assigned it—perhaps we have forfeited our right to dominion?

We must acknowledge the force of this criticism. The biblical tradition itself affirms that human beings long ago began corrupting the earth, in the "generation of the Flood" and the "generation of the dispersion" (who built the Tower of Babel). God declared, after saving Noah and his family from the Flood, that "the imagination of man's heart is evil from his youth" (Gen. 8:21). But God did not despair of humankind and continued to respond to those who sought to live a higher and truer way, from Abraham and Sarah down to the present. The task for human beings today is to live up to higher ideals and to seek continually a higher and more inclusive vision— the perspective of a king saving his kingdom, rather than a narrow and ego-centered point of view.

The emphasis on the visionary powers of human beings comes in an ancient *midrash,* which says that Adam could "see from one end of the world to the other." Adam is compared to the lights of heaven, "to give light on earth" (Gen. 1:14). In other words, Adam, male-and-female, had a complete vision of the divine work and its ultimate purpose. Then Adam was divided into a gendered being, expressing in bodies (but not, Kabbalah tells us, the same kind of bodies we have now) the duality that inheres in this level of creation. When these two beings were expelled from the Garden, their holistic vision was lost.

But we still use the word *vision* to express an awareness of higher purpose. The person who can see wondrous possibilities that have not yet been actualized is called a visionary. Even our concept of the universe as an evolving, magnificent organism depends on the vision of human beings, extended through the scientific instruments that reveal billions of years of space-time or the intricacies of molecular genetic structures. Humans have always sought to expand their capacity to see the purpose of things, seeking wisdom from ancient astrologers, who tried to discern meanings in the movements of stars, or from the speech of prophets and oracles. Today, the subject of cosmology (literally, knowledge of the whole cosmos) is an exciting area for physicists and mathematicians as well as philosophers and theologians, once again in search of the complete vision.

Tiferet-Splendor is the *sefirah* of vision, purpose, and capacity for high-level organization in light of that purpose. Its name suggests the beauty and magnificence of the created being who possesses the vision of creation's purpose. This *sefi-rah* is also called Truth, because it is the place where human perception can meet divine revelation.

These symbolic references reveal the honor and splendor given to human beings who identify themselves with God's ultimate purposes on earth. This is our task as well. But this high place in the scheme of things means also that the fate of the world lies in our hands. We, too, must make sure that all the rungs on the ladder are in place, that our connection to the heavenly template is secure so that we can live a truly good life on earth.

The Heart Connection

What makes it possible for humans, among all animals, to carry the vision? How is it that we have the potential to make the right choices, to energize what will support and magnify the best of life? Kabbalah teaches that it is the human heart.

On the diagram of *sefirot,* Splendor, at the center of the upper torso, is usually associated with the heart and corresponds to the heart chakra in the yogic traditions. It also is a center into which all the upper *sefirot* flow and from which the lower *sefirot* emanate. Furthermore, this heart center in traditional Kabbalah is directly connected to the uppermost *sefirah,* Crown, which points to the essential soul. This tells us that the heart can become a direct expression of the soul. On a personal level, the heart can overflow with soulfulness into the *sefirot* immediately below it, until it is expressed in the human personality and energizes behavior on an everyday basis. On the collective level, human passion, rightly directed, can change the world.

By passion, however, I do not mean emotions. Kabbalah teaches that our ordinary emotions are a function of the lower torso. The heart sustains a higher level: an overriding passion connected to what is meaningful, something great enough to motivate one's entire life. Edmund Hillary, who longed to conquer Mount Everest, and Mother Teresa, who was drawn to comfort the poor and sick, are heroic examples from history. But another is the daughter of one of my friends, whose love for animals led her to volunteer for the SPCA, spending her time caressing abused and abandoned pets. And my student at the university whose passion for soccer drove him so hard that he failed my class.

Yet even these examples of Splendor, our most powerful passions and motivations, are only hints of the larger vision: the ultimate purpose for which everything was created. In the heart is also our deepest understanding—as we saw earlier, *Binah*-Understanding resides in the right side of the heart as well in the brain. We think our deep thoughts in the heart. Thus when the Bible wants to express an important idea forming in the mind of God or of a person, it uses the expression, "he said in his heart."

Rabbi Nachman offers us a beautiful parable of the heart in one of the stories included in his multileveled story "The Seven Beggars":

> There is a mountain. On the peak of the mountain there is a stone. From this stone, there flows a Spring.
>
> Everything has a heart. Therefore the world as a whole also has a heart....
>
> The mountain with the stone and the Spring stands at one end of the world. The Heart of the World stands at the opposite end of the world. The Heart of the World faces the Spring and constantly longs and yearns to come to the Spring. It has a very, very great longing, and it cries out very much that it should be able to come to the Spring. The Spring also yearns for it.

The Heart has two things that make it weak. First, the sun pursues it and burns it. The second thing that weakens the Heart is the great longing and yearning that it constantly has toward the Spring. It longs and yearns so much that its soul goes out, and it cries out.

When it wants to rest a bit and catch its breath, a great bird comes and spreads its wings over it, protecting it from the sun. It can then relax a bit. However, even when it is resting, it looks toward the Spring and yearns for it.

One may wonder, since it yearns for it so much, why does it not go to the Spring? However, if it were to come close to the mountain, then it would no longer see the mountain's peak. It then could not gaze at the Spring, and if it stopped looking at the Spring, it would die, since its main source of life is the Spring....

If the Heart died, then the entire world would cease to exist. The Heart is the life force of all things, and nothing can exist without a heart.[9]

The Spring is the flowing forth of the Divine, represented by the *sefirah* of Wisdom. The Heart, Splendor, has two aspects, both of which take its energy—its yearning for the Spring and the effects of the sun. The yearning is the aspect of the heart connected to Understanding, the mother, who yearns for Wisdom, the father. It is also the indescribable yearning of the human soul for God.

The aspect of the sun in Splendor is the pull of waking consciousness—life under the sun, so to speak—with all its daily tasks, physical needs, and material desires. This is the world in which we all live. Through the energy of Splendor, we carry the sense of purpose that demands we take responsibility for that world. But that responsibility takes its toll on the

Heart. Rabbi Nachman is telling us that the human heart is stretched between the longing for God on the one hand and the pull of responsibility for, and responsiveness to, the world on the other. Yet that tension is exactly where we must live. If the Heart tried to go to the Spring, it would no longer be able to "see the mountain's peak" and "gaze at the Spring." The Heart would lose its visionary capacity, its sense of purpose for life, and it would die.

On the other hand, the Heart becomes exhausted by the world in which it lives. To live under the sun is its true purpose, but it needs the "great bird" to give it respite. The Hasidic commentaries explain that the wings of the bird are like the lungs on both sides of the human heart. Rabbi Nachman taught that the heart produces such internal heat (like a sun) that the lungs are needed right next to the heart to cool it with breathing. The heart is nourished by the breath.

In the Unfolding of Creation, Adam-Humanity represents the Heart of the World, positioned at Splendor among the *sefirot*. With its connection to Understanding, the human heart longs for a higher world. But at the same time it knows that it can only gaze at that world. Gazing is a code word in Hasidic writings for meditation, and it reminds us here of "con-template-ion"—renewing our connection to the basic template of existence. Meditation and contemplation of the vision regenerate the passion the Heart needs to continue beating, maintaining the flow of life.

But the Heart of the World beats not for itself, but for the world as a whole. Indeed, it is so connected to the world that it can be drawn into it too much and "burned" by its desires, as we will see in the next chapter. Still, the Heart must beat—and humans must work for the good of the entire world. To have respite from its work, the lungs offer shade and coolness. This means not only doing spiritual practices like breathing and meditation, which Rabbi Nachman recommends, but also seeing ourselves in a magnificent system of reciprocity, represented by the lungs, which exchange carbon dioxide for oxygen, moment by moment. When we recognize our place in the cosmic story, the grandness of God's creation and the multitude of details, like the amazing mechanics of breathing, that sustain our life, we can appreciate more fully the profound honor we have been given of sustaining life on this planet in return. This quality is what we need to become truly a manifestation of beauty and splendor.

5

DIVINE ACTUALIZATION

Contemplate the wonders of creation, the Divine dimension of their being, not as a dim configuration that is presented to you from a distance, but as the reality in which
you live.

—RABBI ABRAHAM ISAAC KOOK, *LIGHTS OF HOLINESS*

HARNESSING LIFE FORCE:
NETZACH-PERSEVERANCE AND *HOD*-SURRENDER

THE LEVEL OF *TIFERET*-SPLENDOR has the potential to mirror
divinity in this world. From the viewpoint of Kabbalah, from
Splendor upward, humans interact with God and with other
forces greater than humanity. From Splendor downward,
humans strive to direct the world as ambassadors of God, inter-
twining human and divine will. Out of the human potential to
co-create, each generation faces the task of sustaining and caring for the world. By bestowing kindness on all creation,
humanity can actually imitate God.

This task requires harnessing the energies of *Netzach*-
Perseverance and *Hod*-Surrender. These are the *sefirot* of
life force, the energies of survival and procreation. They manifest as desires for food, for sex, and for the means to ensure
those necessities, including power and wealth. They also run

73

parallel to *Chesed*-Expansiveness and *Gevurah*-Restraint as a basic duality.

The expansive energy is called Perseverance, corresponding to Expansiveness. On the level of human civilization, it becomes the drive to achieve and continue, imitating divine expansiveness. Its energy appears in the drive of life to emerge everywhere—tiny plants that peek out between desert rocks, penguins that adapt to the frigid climate of Antarctica. In the human being, perseverance is symbolized by the will to live and to express oneself in relation to one's environment. Some have called it domination because of its emphasis on expansive self-expression. We see Perseverance in the desire to make a mark on the world, to leave behind memorials and monuments testifying to our existence. Our tendency is to fall in love with our own creations, like the story of Pygmalion where a sculptor created the form of a beautiful woman and fell in love with his own statue. This is the negative side of Perseverance. It can become exploitative or manipulative, but we should also remember that it usually contains inherent qualities of love and goodwill because it is from the side of Expansiveness.

In individual human beings, Perseverance is also expressed in the strength of the body, the way the organs and muscles of the body respond to a person's will and put forth effort to carry out his or her wishes.

Its companion *sefirah*, Surrender, parallels the energy of Restraint, expressed now as the inclination to yield and withdraw. As complex organisms develop, the specialization of cells means also that each type of cell is willing to become dependent on others. The symbiosis of plants manifests the ability of life to yield and share resources. In both the animal and plant worlds, each species is able to respond to the presence of others in the same environment.

In the human being, *Hod* has many dimensions. In relation to God and the larger collectivity, it is expressed as the impulse to sacrifice, imitating the divine contraction in "sacrificing" space for the sake of creating a world. As mentioned earlier, in our most ancient stories—Cain and Abel, Noah—and in the most ancient levels of civilization, we find the profound practice of sacrificing what is valuable to the Divine.[1] *Hod*-Surrender also includes willingness to sacrifice ourselves for the larger whole, as in martyrdom or war.

In the individual human being, Surrender means the ability to yield or step back, removing our ego from a situation. It involves the capacity to feel inwardly and process that information in order to sense how things fit together. Surrender also enables us to access information not available to normal consciousness, as when our cells "remember" injury by replicating scar tissue. In its more negative formations, however, this *sefirah* can express itself as negativity, feelings of victimization, or withdrawal from creative interaction with the world.

Out of these powerful energies of Perseverance and Surrender, many things emerge that are beautiful and amazing, for humans are creative in their own right. Families become clans, tribes, societies, civilizations. Prophets and seers bring forth rich visions that guide ritual ceremonies, dances, and martial arts as well as music and visual arts. Technologists invent tools to make life more comfortable and to enhance our experience of creation: a fire pit, a furnace, a hammer and anvil, cast bronze; polished stones, carved stones, jewelry, and ornaments; clay pots, porcelain, glass, and crystal. The cooperative effort of humankind indeed leads to dominion over nature.

Yet these creations are also things to which human beings can become deeply attached, rather than using them to honor God and the larger creative process. Human civilization is a tale of how the effort to build a world of splendor became mostly an effort to garner material goods, fame, progeny, wives, sex, food, or money. Christians called this tendency the sin of pride. Buddhists called it ignorant craving. Jews called it the evil inclination, or misdirected desire. Even secular reconstructions of human prehistory point to a crisis as humans passed from gathering and hunting to agricultural societies, inventing war and empire, and later racism, nationalism, and even genocide.[2]

Why? What is common to all these interpretations is that somehow, in the human psyche, anxiety and fear arose—fear of not being good enough, or of not having enough. Self-doubt and insecurity seem inherent in the human psyche, and its dark mirrors are grandiosity and greed. The Eden story tells us of the serpent who enticed human beings with the thought of being like God—they felt they needed to gain more power even though they were already created in God's image. Existentialist philosophers of the mid-twentieth century captured some of the depth of human fear by calling it "ontological anxiety"—fear of not being. Psychologists sometimes have suggested that this anxiety arises out of the experience of independence itself, as a fear of loss of parental love.

Whatever the origin of the problem, the natural energies of survival, or instincts, became entwined with what psychology later would call ego. Physical productions or contractions became wealth, bodily strength and vitality became power, and the intimate exchanges of man and woman became merely sex or an economically or politically arranged marriage. Shoring themselves up against doubt, humans sought reassurance from the external world. Group identity became a powerful source of security, filling an inner void. But the emphasis on group identification nourished exclusiveness and fragmentation in human society, until finally fear ran the world instead of love. Perseverance and Surrender, the creative energies at our immediate disposal, became the locus of a new problem—not the general problem of pain in the world of duality, but of how human beings create their own suffering.

The energies of the *sefirot* of the lower torso, designed for the concrete and practical application of divine love and discipline using the tools of survival and procreation, became corrupt. They were harnessed to the service of what some Jewish mystics call the "animal soul." Acting primarily from animal instincts of survival and defense, the animal soul battles the divine soul, which seeks to live in accordance with a higher vision. This interpretation is a way of telling us how powerful our egotistical desires have been. Down to the present, Perseverance and Surrender in the human realm are still given over to competitive and ultimately self-devouring processes. In Western culture, which now affects the entire world, Perseverance became predominantly a masculine characteristic, Surrender a feminine one. Instead of being a gracious flow of exchange between heaven and earth, up and down the entire range of the *sefirot,* human energy circles around itself. The whole earth—and, Kabbalah tells us, the heavens too—suffer from our narcissistic fear, which severs our connection to divine vision.

A new unification is needed. Not only do we need to maintain our vision, keeping *Tiferet*-Splendor connected to the higher worlds, but we also need to manage the world in accord with that vision. Perseverance and Surrender have the tendency to separate from their divine source, becoming materialistic and self-worshiping. It is as if the serpent won his point: Now humans think they are like gods. These energies must be organized through the *sefirah* called *Yesod*-Foundation in a way that keeps the connection open to higher levels.

LINEAGE, HISTORY, KARMA: *YESOD*-FOUNDATION

Yesod-Foundation is usually portrayed as the *sefirah* of repro-
duction or, more broadly, generativity and transmission. In the
larger animal and plant world, the process through which this
occurs is primarily genetic. The species' drive to live and
expand its reach (Perseverance) combines with the need to
draw back and respond to others (Surrender), creating an
ecosystem. The ecosystem in turn encourages the development of new forms. Within each, effective strategies for this
eventually become part of the genetic pool, the "foundation"
for the future. In the human realm, Foundation is represented
as the genitals and womb.

But the idea of transmission must embrace far more than
sexuality and genetics. Humans transmit information from their
families and their entire lineage, from society and culture.
Foundation is the place where all that is collectively experienced
is merged and passed on to the next generation. Like the birth
canal, it channels into specific and unique form the multitude of
experiences that any given society has accumulated. Essentially,
it is the divine quality of memory. In some kabbalistic sources,
Foundation is called All, signifying its comprehensiveness.[3]

Since our parental and cultural heritage is available
through Foundation, we can access the merit of the good
deeds of our ancestors. Judaism holds that God counts good as
weighing more than evil: "God remembers kindness for a
thousand generations" (Exod. 33:6–7). Other traditions, such as
Buddhism and Christianity, also speak of a store of merit accumulated by the great acts of figures of the past. We stand, the
Rabbis have said, "on the shoulders of giants." The Jewish
prayers each day include thanks to God, "Who remembers the
devoted acts of our ancestors, and Who brings a redeemer to
their children's children."

Remembering is also "re-member-ing," reuniting the broken pieces. Divine remembrance infuses the *sefirah* of Foundation, because God pieces together and holds the memory of past goodness for us. *Yesod*-Foundation thus enables us to bring into this lifetime a mastery of many good qualities, from all that has been learned and accomplished in the past.

Rewriting the Past

All humans manifest the *sefirah* of Foundation when we pass on a heritage, whether to the next generation or to our contemporaries. We do this in the initiation rites of the generation, but also in the casual stories we tell of our ancestors and our past. The rites of transmission begin in childhood with schooling and continue throughout every passage in adulthood. Such stories and ceremonies are literally the "foundation" for a world that is about to be born with each new generation. They express both the creative spark that is our sense of identity, and our cooperation with others, our sense of being part of a larger whole that is created by the collective, reciprocal work of Perseverance and Surrender.

Today, for the first time ever, the entire world can hear the stories we tell. Through worldwide mass communication and massive interaction of people from different countries and traditions, we do have the possibility of something new emerging. But what most often happens is that we revert to the archetypes of dominance. In a multicultural age, the most common international symbol seems to be that of the superhero who conquers aliens of one sort or another. Should we not be trying to teach instead that no sentient being is alien to us? Further, the public channels of tradition have most often been created and maintained exclusively by males. Surely we must insist that women's perspectives be included, publicly as well as privately, as we formulate our teachings for the next generation.

Most of all, the heritage we pass on through Foundation must be inclusive, connected to wholeness. It must be connected to prophetic vision, which takes history and forges it in accord with a vision of the future. This is the spark that enlivens the passing on of tradition, the continuance of society, the renewal of the past. Some traditions, notably the Hindu and Buddhist, place a great value on what is called "direct transmission." Although Judaism holds that learning in the context of family and community are the valid means of transmitting Torah, the image is useful in conveying the spirit that must infuse learning and community. The direct current that runs from Crown through Foundation is the means by which the energies circling through our social world are purified and refined in light of a higher vision.

In Jewish tradition, prophetic vision and history are intimately related. The history books in the Bible, such as Joshua, Judges, Samuel, and Kings, are part of the collection of the Prophets, just as much as Amos, Hosea, Isaiah, and Jeremiah. Both history and prophecy involve the ability to see the big picture of processes going on in a temporal framework. The prophet is nourished by the fact that his heart is attached to the ideal, "gazing at the Spring," to use Rabbi Nachman's metaphor. Yet there is a difference between what happens in the upper triangle, around *Tiferet*-Splendor, and what happens in the lower triangle, focused at *Yesod*-Foundation. Whereas the energy of the heart is characterized by yearning, that of the lower torso is processing and clarifying. Its guardians are the kidneys, whose main job is refining. Our refining is a reenvisioning of not only our current society but also our traditions, remnants of the visions of previous generations.

Sometimes, our sense of discomfort with the past makes us want to throw out symbols, practices, and beliefs that don't agree with us at the moment. This is not the kind of purification I am suggesting here. What must be refined, in order for the heart's love and the prophet's vision to be passed down to the next generation, is the residue of collective emotion—especially the negative emotions of fear, resentment, humiliation, and desire for domination or revenge. We will learn in Chapter 7 ways of dealing with these emotions on an individual level. Collectively, however, we must recognize that these emotions shape the symbolic frameworks through which we usually interpret everything. All our religions, however elevated and creative their visions, are also clouded by residues of ancient wounds.

In Chapter 2 I spoke of cleaning the sediment out of a glass lamp. The process is nowhere more intense than here. As we become more articulate about what we are striving for—as our gaze into the future and toward the ideal becomes clearer—we work even more assiduously at examining and refining our concepts of the past, which means redefining ourselves.

History shows that human beings do this redefining continually. When a country goes through a political revolution and a new government takes over, suddenly the heroes of the country change. When the Russian Revolution overthrew the czars, city names were changed and statues of revolutionary heroes replaced portraits of emperors; even history textbooks were rewritten. Similarly, when we decide to apply for a different kind of job, we rewrite our résumés to emphasize different relevant experience and background. We remake our past, including all the components of our self-concept, in light of a new vision of the future. This happens not only in an intellectually articulate way, as with résumé writing and school textbooks, but also with ritual, art, and music.

The urgent task now is to reformulate our future and past not in accordance with political needs but by attuning ourselves to spiritual realities: God alive in the world, creativity afoot, with the long-sought unity of the planet, and a desire for the health and well-being of all beings guiding our every move. The model can be taken from the biblical story of Joseph, who reinterpreted what happened to his family. When his brothers were afraid that he might take revenge on them for what they had done to him, he reassured them that God planned all this:

> Now do not be distressed or take it amiss that you sold me into slavery here; it was God who sent me ahead of you to save people's lives.... God sent me ahead of you to ensure that you will have descendants on earth, and to preserve you all, a great band of survivors. So it was not you who sent me here, but God, and He has made me an adviser to Pharaoh and lord over all his household and ruler of all Egypt. (Gen. 45:5–8)

We need to reconnect to the grand design, as Joseph urged his brothers to do. He told the story with an eye to the future and the betterment of humanity—"to save people's lives ... to ensure that you will have descendants." We must retell the story of our planet and the natural world and the story of humankind. In our stories of nature, we must reinstate God and spirit, while at the same time incorporating insights from ecology, seeing ourselves in relation to a diverse and sentient world rather than as dominating nature. Historically, the great stories that have inspired the world must be retold. Jewish tradition, with its great Exodus story, the story of divine redemption from slavery, has inspired liberation movements all over the world. In the past two centuries, women and oppressed minorities have been contributing their own stories to this stream of collective memory. Our stories must "re-member" humanity by speaking of those who have been denied their voice and their access to avenues of influence.

We must tell our own tradition's unique stories with these issues in mind. We must tell stories of creativity, of struggling against odds, of refusing to oppress others, of love and compassion and forgiveness, of people placing divine wholeness and connection to other beings above all else.

And we must tell stories of miracles. We can only break through the vise grip that mechanistic science has on our consciousness by recognizing the role of God in everything. The Baal Shem Tov, founder of Hasidism, taught that no leaf falls without God's willing it. Each of us experiences amazing events—from coincidences to clear miracles—in our lives. We must see the Divine acting in all these and have the courage to tell those stories. When we do, we will see that the billiard-ball causation of the old mechanistic science is not the only force in the universe. God is in our midst, with the force of cohesion rather than mere causation, bringing people and events together for an ultimate good. "God sent me before you."

The statement of Joseph is so fitting because it puts events in the right perspective: Each person has done his part; the end result is up to God. All that we have done, all that we have attempted, all that we have learned is not ours but God's. Whatever we thought or hoped or expected might happen from our individual and social efforts, the ultimate result is out of our hands.

Like the belly of a woman in her last few weeks of pregnancy, *Yesod*-Foundation is heavy with potential and difficult to carry. At this point, we recognize the enormous responsibility we have to be channels for a reformulation of perspective. We must take everything in heaven and earth and add our own creative spark to transmit to the world. When we are aware that Foundation is the transmission of divine will that began at Crown, we can express our gratitude and move forward with freedom.

BRINGING ENERGY INTO FORM: MALKHUT-MANIFESTATION

Divine energy has constellated itself in many transformations, through each of the *sefirot*. This energy now results in something: what exists. Present existence is *Malkhut*-Manifestation. Normally it is all that we see and hear and touch. All the other levels are invisible. They are, as Kabbalah says, hidden worlds.

Malkhut-Manifestation is our ordinary life, lived on the thin skin of a world while great events surge beneath. The empty feeling of "What am I doing here?" comes up when we have skimmed along the surface for too long. The human being is meant to explore, to go beyond mere appearances. From the time that ancient astronomers asked why the moon appears at a different time every night and contemplative souls delved into the darkness of the human psyche, we have been trying to decipher the mysteries. Judaism insists, however, that mere contemplation of mysteries, or even personal experience of them, is not enough. The insights and knowledge we receive must be used to transform the world. This happens in the *sefirah* of Manifestation.

Only in the arena of Manifestation can we complete the circuit of thought, emotion, speech, and action. When we consciously act, we make changes in the physical world through actual contact with it, or we set vibrations in motion with our speech. In this way, truly new things come into being. We think, we organize, and finally we speak and act. Our "decrees" become reality. The capacity to initiate decrees and have them carried out—to introduce a new will into the world—is kingship, the literal meaning of the Hebrew word *malkhut*. In Kabbalah, Manifestation means that our true intent, whether unconscious or conscious, reaches completion. In Rabbi Nachman's story of the turkey prince, Manifestation is restoring ourselves to our true noble essence, like the prince once again sitting at the banquet table.

The truth of the realm of Manifestation is that we will bring everything we know and feel into actualized reality in some form. Humans have the gift of being able to be conscious of the depths of being and experience them. One of the amazing adventures of humanity in the past two hundred years is the discovery of undreamed levels of existence: the mysteries of the genetic code, the forces within the atom, distant stars and black holes. Will we exercise conscious, ethical control over our knowledge of other dimensions of existence? Will we ask what God wants us to do with it? Will we consider the larger implications of our actions? Or will we follow the most enjoyable or profitable path and leave the results to chance?

Problems arise when, at this final point of action, we have separated ourselves off from the whole. For example, we know we have a responsibility to vote in elections. The template on which democratic societies are based is expressed in the will of the people and the equality of all citizens. In the United States, these principles are seen as divinely sanctioned in their origins. Social institutions are set up to regulate our interactions, in accord with that original high intent, but the correspondence between the original divine will and the society we live in depends on, among other things, our vote.

We will, hopefully, prepare ourselves by studying the candidates' past records and their positions on important issues. Through this effort, and then casting our votes, we issue our "decrees" to be considered with all the others who vote. Normally, we just accept the results. But sometimes we suddenly become attached to the outcome. For example, in the American presidential contest in 2000, apparently rational people became intensely partisan. They stopped listening to others and stopped being self-critical. Instead of thinking about the process as a whole, they fixated on one particular version of reality, rooted in their own egos' perception of themselves and their place in the universe. This is a temptation that occurs all the time at the level of Manifestation: to build ourselves a rigid little universe in which we insist on being the star players.

How do we correct this rigidity? One way is to remember that responsibility is not something that can belong to a person ("it's *my* responsibility"). Responsibility is the ability to respond, which implies a larger context, a community, a world of other actors and thinkers, and God as a major player too, with intricate processes linking heaven to earth. This is the Jewish concept of covenant. We are all responsible for one another and to one another. You may be a prince or princess, given dominion over your part of the world, but you live in a larger world of nobility, including a divine king who is intimately involved.

It is also important to respect processes for decision making that are designed to include many different factors and arrive at a balanced decision. This is the final guidance of the arrow to its exact place on the target. Judicial and legislative procedures are the most common such processes in secular society. In religious traditions, values and principles (such as those enshrined in law) are usually combined with the insight and compassion of spiritual leaders. In Judaism, for example, there is a process by which one decides every action: *halacha,* literally "the walking," the general term for applied Jewish law. Built on the deliberations of sages over three thousand years, and in many historical eras and cultures, *halacha* defines how a person can walk rightly in the world.[4] Not every Jew today accepts traditional *halacha* as binding authority, but the concept of a way to walk with integrity and responsibility runs throughout Judaism, and similar ideas appear in every truly spiritual path. A way of responsibility must mark Manifestation—a way of responding collectively as well as individually to the divine intent. Then *Malkhut*-Manifestation becomes the mirror of *Keter*-Crown, not only in vision but also in reality.

FOLLOWING THE RULE

Every lasting religious community has its rule, its path of responsibility. The Eightfold Noble Path of Buddhism insists on right ways to act, speak, and earn a living, as well as how to follow a spiritual intent and meditate. In medieval European monasteries, such guidelines were called the *regula,* Latin for "rule," as in "the Rule of Saint Benedict." Interestingly, this word probably comes from the Hebrew word *regel,* which means foot—the part of the body that walks (as in *halacha*). Although every general rule has many specific rules, each tradition conveys the sense that the details relate to an overarching concept of how to live the best possible life. In the Western religions, the concept of a rule is related to the concept of a God who reveals divinity to the world. The rule is the manifestation of divine will, to the extent that human beings can understand it. In many Native American traditions, there is the concept of a way. Judaism says, "The way of the earth is the foundation of Torah," meaning that the ethical rules and codes of civility recognized by all humanity are basic rules for Jews as well. On those general ethical principles is built the further, more detailed path of *halacha.* The rule in each religion usually urges people to a higher path than is prescribed by society at large. In each religion there is also another, still more demanding kind of path, a personal path that must be blazed by each individual.[5]

Today we live in a time when people often reject rules and laws, in Judaism and elsewhere. Living according to a rule passed down by tradition seems superficial.

Malkhut-Manifestation has lost its connection to the processes that gave rise to it. In the villages and towns of traditional societies, the rule was alive. People were able to feel connected to the process of setting specific rules through their social networks and their leaders. From the point of view of the *sefirot,* we can say that the families, clans, and respected teachers of the community's heritage embodied Foundation. The righteous one in Judaism, the saint in Christianity, or the guru in Hinduism embodied Splendor, and the mystic represented the possibility of access to yet higher realms. Their guidance, decision making, and examples of personal discipline ensured that Manifestation with its rules was intimately connected to all the levels of divine creation and revelation. But to modern individuals, living without a vibrant religious society, organized religion may seem to consist only of alien rules and empty rituals. Living by the rules alone feels like going into a museum that has been looted of its treasures. Entire galleries are empty; paintings have been ripped out of their frames.

Our concern about superficiality and rote practice is not only a result of modernity. Mystics in all traditions preached to people about spiritual emptiness. They knew that human society, including its religion, sometimes lost its connection to the upper worlds. They wanted desperately for people to live from inside—not to break the rules, but to reach the heart of the tradition within the rules, where the life and the spirit are. Even in a very religious society, people could become dependent on others for their connection to God, and that society could forget who God really was. Sufis criticized Islamic legalism, Martin Luther fulminated against a church that defined salvation in terms of "works," the Taoists of China criticized the sterility of Confucian society. In Judaism, the prophets, the rabbis of the Talmud, and all the mystics urged that we put our heart into our observances. The message of the mystics is: Find your own connection to *Tiferet*-Splendor and beyond. Learn from society and your teachers, and at the same time know that you need not be merely an imitation of them. Know that you, too, can be an agent of transmission, of *Yesod*-Foundation; you, too, are a prince, an ambassador of God in the world of *Malkhut*-Manifestation. But a prince does not set out to overthrow the rules; rather, he or she *exemplifies them in their noblest form.*

Perhaps we can expand on an ancient Zen teaching that says that if you see someone pointing at the moon, you shouldn't mistake the finger for the moon. In the case of religion, this means don't mistake the rules of religion for ultimate reality or God. On the other hand, if you are looking for the moon—or, to use a better analogy, trying to find a constellation in the sky—you would be a fool to ignore the finger pointing you in the right direction. The finger that points is the rule, with all its implications.

The rule is, in short, a measure by which we live. Its specifics are the result of the cooperation of divine and human intent, down through the ages, filtered through all the conditions of nature and human society. This perspective assumes that the vast majority of the rules and laws in modern societies are good and life enhancing. Like laws of nature (which we also now understand have evolved over time[6]), the greater the diversity of situations in which they have survived, providing for both continuity and creativity, the more fundamental they are to the human project. That is one reason why Judaism, like most traditions, has changed its rules very slowly over time.[7]

It is possible within Judaism to have what is called "an argument for the sake of heaven"—differences of opinion based not on our own desires, but on the sincere conviction, based on deep knowledge of tradition, that a certain course of action is or is not in accord with the divine will. Yet Jewish mystics have always insisted that we can't break the laws and still achieve spiritual freedom. We may feel that we have risen above the need to do exactly as the laws of society or religion dictate, but that feeling usually comes from egotistical perception, not spiritual insight. Most important, any consideration of revising the rules must come from a place of unification and compassion, not an "us versus them" perspective. Otherwise, we will generate yet more conflict and suffering.

In Judaism the rules themselves often have mystical significance. Kabbalah teaches that if one focuses intensely on a divine commandment, one can achieve higher levels of spirituality. When the *Sefer Yetzirah* comments, "They rush to His saying like a whirlwind" (1:6), Rabbi Aryeh Kaplan adds, "The fact that [the mystic] is pursuing a Divine 'saying' allows him to have access to much higher states of consciousness than he normally can attain. It is for this reason that many mystics would engage in meditations related to the observances of various commandments."[8] Similarly, the *Tanya* teaches that performing a commandment is a way to unite directly with the divine will—it is, in essence, a mystical act.[9] By putting our will at the service of the Divine, we reduce the scope of the ego, which typically asks us to rationalize our actions in service of our self-interest.

There are two general rules on which, so far as I know, all spiritual teachers agree. One is doing good and giving to our fellow human beings, especially to those in need. The work of serving others is the most universal way to eliminate ego. Moreover, in Jewish mysticism, acts of goodness are the basis of what is called the "arousal from below"—human action that will in turn stimulate God to shower divine love on earth. As Rabbi Schneur Zalman of Liadi wrote near the turn of the nineteenth century, on the eve of the technological and ideological revolutions that were to transform world culture, compassionate action is the crucial thing:

After the creation of "man to work on it" [the earth], every arousal from above, to arouse the attribute of the Supreme Expansiveness, depends on an arousal from below, that is, *the charity and kindness that we do in this world* ... in these times ... the principal service of God is the service of charity.[10]

The other virtually universal rule is to set aside time for your relationship to God. In Judaism, this essential aspect of spirituality has been instituted through insistence on the collective and personal observance of Shabbat (the Sabbath), which has been admired and sometimes adapted by many in other spiritual traditions.[11] But whether or not you take on a Sabbath, a substantial amount of sacred time is a crucial part of spiritual practice.

Malkhut-Manifestation is traditionally represented by King David, for the Hebrew letters of his name signify "empty and empty" or "poor and poor," holding nothing to himself. As David represents the human being as servant of God, his name stands in contrast to a certain enemy of God, in a war that Ezekiel prophesies will occur in the future (Ezek. 38). This enemy is named Gog, the letters of which mean "full and full," that is, full of himself even after having been shown the reality of God. Spiritually, this speaks of the ultimate war between the one who nullifies himself before the infinite and the one who hold onto his ego. When that war is over, the ultimate manifestation, known as the Kingdom of God, will be complete.

We will now turn to exploring how to implement a kabbalistic understanding of the world from a more personal perspective. But first, here are the *sefirot* as I have described them in the Unfolding of Creation, for review:

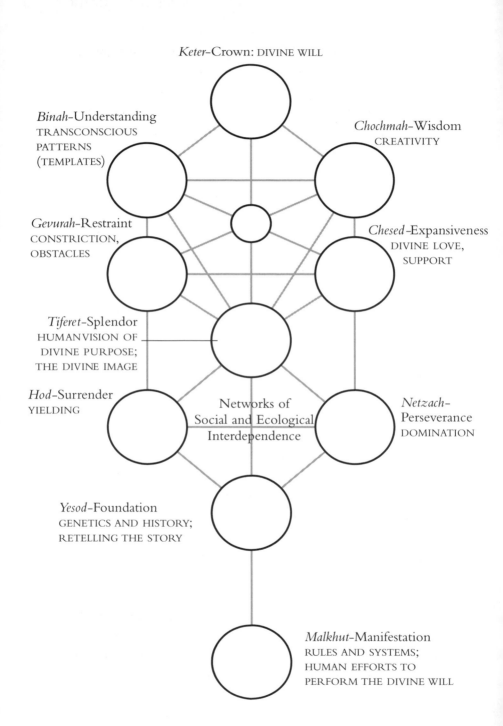

Keter-Crown: DIVINE WILL

Binah-Understanding
TRANSCONSCIOUS
PATTERNS
(TEMPLATES)

Chochmah-Wisdom
CREATIVITY

Gevurah-Restraint
CONSTRICTION,
OBSTACLES

Chesed-Expansiveness
DIVINE LOVE,
SUPPORT

Tiferet-Splendor
HUMAN VISION OF
DIVINE PURPOSE;
THE DIVINE IMAGE

Hod-Surrender
YIELDING

Networks of
Social and Ecological
Interdependence

Netzach-
Perseverance
DOMINATION

Yesod-Foundation
GENETICS AND HISTORY;
RETELLING THE STORY

Malkhut-Manifestation
RULES AND SYSTEMS;
HUMAN EFFORTS TO
PERFORM THE DIVINE WILL

PART III

THE PATH OF
REMEMBERING

6

CLEARING THE PATH

Ben Zoma says, Who is wise? He who learns from every person, as it is said, "From all my teachers I grew wise" (Psalm 119:99).

Who is strong? He who subdues his personal inclination, as it is said, "He who is slow to anger is better than the strong man, and a master of his passions is better than a conqueror of a city" (Proverbs 16:32).

Who is rich? He who is happy with his lot, as it is said, "When you eat of the labor of your hands, you are praiseworthy and all is well with you" (Psalm 128:2) ...

Who is honored? He who honors others, as it is said, "For those who honor Me I will honor, and those who scorn Me shall be degraded" (1 Samuel 2:30).
—MISHNAH, *PIRKE AVOT* 4:1

EXAMINING OUR PERSONAL HISTORY

KABBALAH SAYS THAT WE ARE the thousands of mirrors of the one God. How can we realize this awareness in our lives? How can we know, through all the world's turmoil and strife, the love and beauty that God wants to manifest within us? We do it by filling *Malkhut*-Manifestation—ordinary existence—with divine reality, clearing all the sediment from the lamp so that light can shine all the way through from *Keter*-Crown.

Understanding and contemplating the *sefirot,* as we have begun to do in Part II, is the first step. We now have a map of divine reality seen from a cosmic perspective, from the process of creation to the way that humans try to manifest the divine will in society. Now we can use that information to reconstruct upward, from *Malkhut* to *Keter.*

We begin by addressing our personal history as it manifests in the lower *sefirot*—Manifestation, Foundation, Surrender, and Perseverance. From a spiritual point of view, each individual's personal history is an adventure of the soul. Often we perceive successful people's biographies as paradigmatic, while we think of others' (our own? our family's?) as tales of failures and wrong turns interspersed with accomplishments of which society approves. Then we agonize over the past or feel victimized. The spiritual process of Kabbalah takes a different direction. We want to discover the truest sense of ourselves—our connection back to our original source. And then we want to let the light of that source flow through us completely, as though we were empty vessels.

As we are growing up, we rarely see ourselves as vessels of divinity. In the world of the turkey prince under the table, we experience ourselves as dependent on the goodwill of others. Unlike most animals, we do not have the abilities we need to sustain our own lives. We need a long period to become full human beings. During that period, we are involved in innumerable exchanges with the other beings in our lives, exchanges that offer us opportunities to define our lives. But we don't really know enough to make conscious choices for most of that time. We reach adulthood still entangled in the energies of childhood and adolescence—the social energies that, as we saw in Chapter 5, are embedded in the four lowest *sefirot*.

We must disentangle ourselves in order to live our soul's mission effectively. The most important aspects of that disentanglement are to recognize how our identities have come into being and how our ties to the past hinder us.

EGO AND NAMING

First we identify our attachments to our egos. The ego is connected to the roles we play in life and to our current version of our personal identity. This attachment begins very early in life, when the society we live in gives us a name.

Recall that the lowest of the ten *sefirot,* Manifestation, is the world just as we ordinarily see it. Divine energy is present but quite concealed. Physically, this world operates according to natural laws and is socially constructed by our culturally determined perceptions. These natural and social constraints constitute "the rule," as described in Chapter 5. When children are born, they are immediately given a place in this world—a role. The role fits them into the rule of society.

The action by which this is done is the naming of the baby. Names are the signature of the *sefirah* of Manifestation. The first act of Adam in the Bible, the act that completed creation, was to name the animals. Hasidic teacher Rabbi Yitzchak Ginsburgh observes that "Adam ... drew the full experience of life into 'every living creature' by calling it by name."[1] Personal names are a gift the world bestows on us, usually from our parents and close relatives, who thereby assign us a place in the world. We soon learn to respond to our names differently from any other word we hear. We become identified with the name: I *am* David, I *am* Sarah. This identification is the external formation that is associated with the personality we call the ego.

By choosing a particular name, those who named us had already created an image of who we were. Perhaps we were named after ancestors, to place us in a lineage. Many cultures have rules that dictate what names can and cannot be given; for example, Ashkenazi Jews do not usually name after a living relative, but frequently after a deceased one. Other cultures have restrictions about certain names, for example, names of people who died in unusual ways. In some societies, it is considered a good thing to name after the parent, so that we find John Sr. and John Jr., or even Richard I, II, and III. Sometimes, parents are creative with names, inventing new ones or taking rarely used ones for their new baby. Sometimes parents say that they saw something about this baby that led them to give him or her a particular name. Often in American culture, it's just "I always liked that name," which tells us something about the importance of personal whim in our culture!

The importance of the name becomes clear when we observe how children struggle with the name they are given, usually during late childhood or adolescence. They will cherish nicknames given by their friends—or hate them. They will play with their signatures or with the spelling of their given name, trying to get exactly the right style. It is as if the ego that manifested in the world when they were born can no longer hold their energy; it has to be adapted and enlarged in some way.

As adults, we sometimes change our names. Women have traditionally taken on their husband's last name, signifying that they will take on the task of caring for his lineage. Frequently, married women will sign documents with both their birth name and married name: Jane Smith Jones, for example, rather than Jane Louise Jones. They are saying, perhaps unconsciously, that they are bearers of both lineages. A change in religion frequently brings a change in name, or an additional or "secret" name. Moving into a new society often initiates a name change, usually to be more acceptable among one's new associates. Immigrants to the United States often changed their original names to make them easier for English speakers to pronounce. Equally often, customs officers changed the name for them, and the new arrivals decided to accept it.

All this playing with names is a symptom of the process of trying to fit a soul into an ego, a cultural construct. But this world-stage reality is only one level—what Kabbalah alludes to as the *sefirah* of Manifestation. On this level, we are like actors on a stage, each with a part to play, and the entire system of education in every culture teaches us what that part is. We may be creative and we are undoubtedly unique, but at the level of Manifestation, people will always see us in different roles—parent, child, teacher, friend, businessperson, artist—which social rules or structures determine.

Seeing the discrepancy between your assigned role and your inner sense of self is the first step in maturity. Young children don't question their place; they respond to their names, imitate their elders, and diligently acquire social skills. Sometimes they are still fairly young when they begin to feel uncomfortable about who they are. They may say, as one of my children did when she was five, "I'm the worst kid in the world"—an expression of her inner sense that her ego-persona was not her true self. Such an intuition can come out as a wild scream: "I don't fit in! I'm a terrible person!" Children may withdraw or become socially disruptive. They flit from one group to the next, or hold desperately to their small clique of friends. They are discovering that the ego is not all there is. By the time of adolescence or early adulthood, they are often ready to shake up the world, or at least their corner of it, to let us know about this discrepancy—what they often call hypocrisy.

Yet as we mature, we may find that it is not necessary to change our roles radically or overthrow all the rules. Our light can shine from where we are. From time to time, we read stories in the newspaper about amazing people hidden away in various corners of the globe who have lived a long, contented, and admirable life without ever going more than ten miles from where they were born. While this is almost unimaginable to those of us who take airplane journeys of thousands of miles for a week's vacation, such lives speak a profound truth. While we feel we have to travel the world to achieve self-fulfillment, the desire to travel is actually a metaphor for a deeper desire—the inner desire to expand the reach of our soul.

Similarly, in our spiritual development we are really trying to find our "divine name." Earlier, we discussed how the *sefirot* themselves are connected to the power of various divine names, and each name is a manifestation of God. Since each of us is also a manifestation of God, "in the divine image," we also have divine names. We change names as we grow because we are searching.

The first thing to explore, then, is your given name. Perhaps your soul engineered the choice. Jewish mysticism holds that when a person is given a Hebrew name, that name contains a secret of the person's true identity. If you were named for an ancestor, find out as much about that person as possible. List the names you have had since birth. Besides your obvious names, include nicknames, pet names used by certain relatives, tags you didn't like, fantasy names that you thought you might adopt. If you could choose a new name today, what would it be? Ask yourself what each of these names represents to you. Becoming more aware of your name(s) and the whole naming process will help you understand where you have been and where you are going.

THE PAST AND ITS PRESENCE

What else were we given? Scientifically, we now recognize that the DNA in each cell encodes the physical information necessary for growing an entire human being with a unique physical constitution, emotional temperament, and intelligence. Our DNA is a combination of the genes from our two biological parents. Since these genes come from their union, the genetic heritage is appropriately represented by the *sefirah* connected with procreation and transmission of tradition, the *sefirah* of Foundation.

Genetics is not the only determinant, however. Science can show us which parent a gene came from, but it remains a mystery why the genes combine in the particular way they do—why one child in a family is tall and another is short, why one has brown eyes and another blue. Judaism teaches that God is behind this process. God is the third party in the creation of every child, and the divine design appears in the unique combinations that individuals receive.

Now, according to Jewish mystical teaching, the soul's mission is to reveal itself. We may have more than one life to do this; the challenges that were not met, the work that was not accomplished in one life, will be offered to the person again, in another form and through different sets of circumstances.[2] According to Kabbalah, the results of past lives—our accomplishments and failures—are encoded in our bodies. The great eighteenth-century thinker known as the Vilna Gaon (R. Eliyahu Kramer, 1720–1797) held that the unique possibilities and limitations of the physical body derive from one's previous life or lives. In effect, the way our genes affect our physical constitution, temperament, or mental abilities may be related to the ways we lived previously. In Jewish teachings, the transmission of such qualities is more than a mechanical process; it is

101

part of the design of a loving God. If indeed the challenges we must face are imprinted in our bodies—our physical body, our emotional temperament, and our mental abilities—these gifts provide a key to what we have to do in this life.

No wonder the *sefirah* related to this process is called *Yesod*-Foundation—it is the "foundation" built in previous lives. Think of all the things we now know are heavily influenced by inherited characteristics—channeled through our parents, perhaps "selected" through our past-life actions: our characteristic voice and walk. Tendencies to strength on the one hand, or weakness on the other, in various areas of body and mind. Talents in art, music, or physical activity. Extroversion and introversion. Each of these, and many more, are gifts to us, through which we will in turn transmit our spiritual gifts to the world. The *sefirah* of Foundation is the creative channel through which the divine light enters and transforms the physically based genetic heritage.

This perspective helps us to understand our mission in life more deeply. We don't need to change ourselves in external ways, whether through cosmetics, accumulating goods, or seeking honor. We can work with what is immediately before us, with us, and in us, and thus reveal the divine light hidden within our own being, this particular and unique form.

Even more important, the encoding from the past includes the positive qualities we have inherited, whether through our own past actions or the merits of our ancestors. As we saw earlier, the Bible teaches that God remembers goodness for a thousand generations, while God recompenses evil for only three or four (Exod. 33:6–7). The Hebrew word for generations, *toledot,* shares the same root as the word for birth, *ledah.* We can understand this as meaning that all the good we have done accumulates and is preserved from the many lives that preceded us. The "bad" is, perhaps, what we are continuing to work on from more recent lifetimes. The "thousand generations" of goodness crystallizes in the endowment we are given at birth and becomes a source of strength.

At the same time, we know that this endowment must be refined and cultivated so that it becomes a useful instrument in our hands, not a wild energy. The Talmud says of King David that he was destined to shed blood, but it was up to him whether he would become a murderer, a warrior, a ritual slaughterer of meat, or a ritual expert in circumcision. He became a warrior on behalf of his people. With all of us, certain qualities will be encouraged by society; our religious heritage can offer a higher vision and a good personal discipline to help us refine our talents. Still, the crucial work has to be done on our own.

CHOOSING COMPANIONS

The next set of energies we must transform on the personal level are the dynamic pair of *sefirot* known as *Netzach*-Perseverance and *Hod*-Surrender. Kabbalah calls them the Companions, those who accompany us on our spiritual path. However, we have many companions long before we realize we are on a spiritual path—all the other people we encounter who affect us.

When the kabbalistic Tree of Life is portrayed on the body, the *sefirot* of Perseverance and Surrender are the legs, from the hips to the knees and heels. As such, they are our support systems. Socially, they represent the way our families, tribes, and communities serve us as we are growing up—guiding, advising, and protecting us. Perseverance and Surrender also represent ways of giving and receiving, the reciprocal relations that constitute family, community, society, and even the larger natural environment.

While the legs and heels are peripheral to the body, and indeed a person can survive physically without them, the energy of Perseverance and Surrender also carry divine energy, bringing in the influences we need to carve out our particular destiny. Still, it is important to remember that while social influences are powerful, they are not determinative. They are interacting with us. We have choices. Our relation to Perseverance and Surrender, therefore, is different from our relation to Manifestation, which, as discussed above, represents the social context in its givenness. As the kabbalists often repeat, "*Malkhut* has nothing of its own." Infants have no control over who their parents are, whether they will be raised by their birth parents or not, whether they will live in a stable home or a dysfunctional one, whether they will live in one place or move frequently.

Yet *how* we respond to these influences, how we select and attract or resist and repel aspects of society, is crucial. Those responses are the individual's work with the forces of Perseverance and Surrender. That work colors and enriches our dominant emotional energies. For example, even young children can resist and protest their circumstances; they can choose a small group of friends from the dozens of other children they meet; they can cling to a special teacher or an aunt or uncle more than their parents. As a child, I identified with one particular aunt out of about thirty aunts, uncles, and older cousins. At that time, my favorite aunt was a kind of black sheep in the family (or so I thought from a child's perspective), living a more adventurous life than anyone else. Since she moved frequently and had settled in exotic California by the time I was a teenager, I rarely saw her, but I resonated with her memory. I allowed and embraced her influence on my life, integrating it into my own inner self-formation.

Perseverance has the quality of expansiveness—it stands on the same side of the Tree of Life as the *sefirah* by that name—because it is our active embracing of alternatives. We say an internal yes to the situation or person presenting itself. Sometimes our choice is even more active—taking the initiative and exerting our will, trying to control a situation, thus this *sefirah* is traditionally called Victory. The clubs we join, the sports we play, and the music we listen to all nurture the emerging self.

The other side, Surrender, is that of withdrawal and restraint. A child has to accept certain social forms as part of his or her life. Family and cultural customs, tribal heritage, styles and fashions—in everything from clothing and home decoration to how we manage relationships—surround us daily. Yet, we can perform our own small contraction, saying an internal no, withdrawing our energy from the activities and relationships we dislike. We surrender externally and restrain ourselves internally. This restraint teaches us, in the larger world, not to be swept away by the crowd. It is our own inner "glory"—the literal meaning of Surrender.

Depending on our temperament and our stage in development, one or the other side may be easier for us. At the college I attended decades ago, 90 percent of the student body joined fraternities or sororities. I found it offensive that during the selection process, many girls were hurt by others' judgments, and I refused to join. I found it more in accordance with my inner truth to say no. One of my sweetest friends, however, was a sorority girl through and through—she had thrown herself into the current of the society and taken a part in shaping it. Neither of us was wrong, but she was playing Perseverance in relation to the given social structure, while I was adopting the position of Surrender.

These two *sefirot* are in constant alternation and mutual interaction. Like our two legs when we walk, they work in tandem to go in a certain direction. We are always developing the "legs" we need to walk. Through the friends we choose, Perseverance and Surrender shape us in new ways. Choosing our companions becomes increasingly important as we develop spiritually. Judaism advises people to make their home a place for Torah scholars to come and teach and never to sit among "scoffers" who ridicule such higher pursuits.[3] Great masters in all traditions describe how they had to leave behind the companions of their youth to have the right support for their higher endeavors. Sufi masters traditionally went wandering, not for sights of this world but to find kindred souls. Christians throughout history created spiritual fellowships, from medieval Catholic devotional circles to eighteenth-century Methodist class meetings. Kabbalah speaks often of secrets shared among the Companions. The implicit teaching is that your Companions should be those who can mirror to you the true divinity of your nature.

You can probably see in your own life how your friendships have tended to change as you focused more on spiritual matters. Are there people you know who are on a spiritual path with whom you would like to associate more often? If so, seek them out. If not, pray that God will bring such people to you.

TRANSFORMING EMOTIONAL TIES

Now let's go one level deeper. In our personal history, the choices we made and the people to whom we felt attracted gave form to our unique emotional and physical being. These networks of reciprocity left an imprint on the various levels of our soul, but particularly on the vital life force that is most deeply connected to the *sefirot* of Perseverance and Surrender.

We are, as we say, *emotionally tied* to the important events and people of our past. It is as if we have been spinning energy fibers out of our emotional selves that attach us to people, groups, and events.[4] Some of these energy connections are help-ful; some impede us as we try to move further. All of them have to be transformed and elevated, or in some cases disconnected.

There seems to be no parallel in the animal world to the wide range and subtlety of emotions experienced and described by humans. In addition to the variety of words we have for emotions, works of art and music elicit and, in a sense, "paint" our emotional range. As we enter any new situation, or even imagine ourselves in a different context, energy runs through the body to inform us of our multilayered response to various possibilities. For example, if we think of going shop-ping for gifts, different emotions will be aroused than if we imagine going to the dentist. All our past experiences of gift shopping and dentistry "move" us, for emotions are "e-motions," movements out of our core self. Because they develop in interaction with the environment, we may tend to blame our upbringing or our society for our reactions. But Judaism, along with many spiritual traditions, teaches us that we can attain a perspective from which we can master them.

Our body stores a vast range of emotional responses, as modern therapies have discovered. We often find that certain kinds of physical treatments (acupuncture, movement therapy, hands-on bodywork) sometimes release old memories. In 1998, I went to my doctor, a movement therapist, for one of a series of treatments for a shoulder injury. We were also explor-ing some chronic back pain. To release some of the tension in my back, he asked me to stand on a small rocking platform and practice keeping my balance. After a little practice, I stepped off the platform and felt a great relaxation and lightness in my knees. Suddenly, a memory of a kind of sweet sadness washed over me. My mind then flipped back to 1964, when a beloved friend told me goodbye on the steps of my college dormitory. I was amazed. I had not entirely forgotten my friend's leaving school, but I had completely erased the memory of those feelings until this simple exercise unlocked the emotion buried in my knees.

Conversely, emotional experiences have physical results. For example, fear with its instinctive fight-or-flight response is, in humans, sometimes translated into anxiety. Sustained anxiety then affects the heart, circulation, and hormonal levels. People who undergo deep trauma as children may carry a set of physical and emotional responses that dominate their entire lives. For example, over the years I have met many people who survived the Nazi Holocaust as children in hiding. Many of them had learned that the best way to deal with any threat was to disappear—to close down all reactions and go into complete silence. As a result, in difficult situations their normal personalities would change, unexpectedly, into stony withdrawal. All of us have such survival strategies, though not usually so extreme.

Jewish mysticism, along with many other spiritual traditions, recognized the danger of carrying negative emotions. Scholarly rabbis, Zen masters, and Christian monks all agree that passions such as anger, lust, and melancholy (what we call depression) are hindrances on the spiritual path, while love and joy are positive influences. The question is, how can we overcome our negative tendencies and create a satisfying, emotionally healthy life? We can work in two complementary ways, corresponding to the *sefirot* of Perseverance and Surrender.

Netzach-Perseverance is the energy of building. It is "motional" and motivational, energizing us to create the enduring structures of our bodies and initiating external responses. As we mature, our capacity to observe both these energies develops more fully, and we can see our impulses and emotions without judging them. Perseverance builds experiences that are conducive to good emotional habits. For example, we can decide to do things that will generate positive feelings: call a friend, go for a walk, change into clothes we really like, make order in a messy room. By choosing spiritual reading material, going to places that inspire us, and being around people we admire for their depth and sensitivity, we can add spirituality to our emotional life. We can make time to study or to meditate. All these are active practices. Judaism has always taught that by *doing,* one eventually integrates the characteristics of *being*—that is, of becoming the kind of person one wants to be.[5] This is the beginning of every deeper phase of spiritual work: building an external framework, a stronger vessel that can receive and hold inspiration.

Hod-Surrender is the way we experience the currents of feeling that run through our bodies in response to our external environment and/or our own thoughts. It is also the energy that enables us to feel acceptance and gratitude (*hoda'ah* in Hebrew is related to thanksgiving) and to let go of attachments. This *sefirah* enables us to observe, learn about, and disconnect ourselves from emotional ties. We use this energy when we exercise restraint on our expression of emotions— outbursts of anger or anxiety, for example. Surrender also helps us see that the original energy of an emotion was information about our environment—for example, a first impression of a person. We can be grateful for that experience and yet reconsider it in a more objective light, and gradually reduce its effects on us.

Just as your legs work in tandem to keep you on track and in balance, the external changes that you make in your life will work along with the internally oriented practices. Usually you won't even need to monitor this balance actively—they require each other, and you won't be able to move far ahead with only one leg. It is certainly the case that if you work with these *sefirot,* your life will change. Whatever your physical age, you will now enter spiritual adulthood.

COLLECTIVE DEMONS AND THEIR VICTIMS

Although the patterns examined here are largely personal, it is important to add a word or two about the collective aspects of the *sefirot* of Perseverance and Surrender, because they often impact our personal lives. You probably have noticed that some people carry wounds that are so deep that it seems impossible for them to heal. Some people seem "possessed" by rage, grief, or a grandiose self-image. All too frequently these states lead to violence against the self or others, or to extreme exploitation of others.

Even if we do not suffer in this way personally, any of us may unexpectedly find ourselves in a relationship with someone like this—an abusive parent, a distraught sibling, a spouse who turns out to have a dark side, or a person to whom we have turned for teaching or guidance but who has become exploitative. When we see mass movements that lead people into grotesque behavior, from the Nazi movement of wartime Germany to late-twentieth-century suicide cults, we can be fairly certain that the leader or leaders are deeply wounded individuals. Those who follow are inescapably affected, though not usually to the same degree.

Sometimes individuals suffer from deep personal trauma, but sometimes they carry the wounds of a generations-old family system or even an entire nation. As a general rule, if we're part of the wounded system—the family or the intimate social group of a wounded person—we should not try to become healers of the individuals involved. Specially trained outsiders may be able to help. We can be compassionate while at the same time remembering to protect ourselves from any direct harm.

Yet we are also being called to a different response of our own. When we find ourselves in a system containing grievous wounds, we are being asked to examine our connection to the larger collective. Do we have habits of thought and speech, patterns of action and reaction, that maintain dysfunctional families from generation to generation? How does our ethnic heritage or religion perpetuate wounds that families and nations may carry? On Ash Wednesday in 2000, Pope John Paul II and the cardinal of the Diocese of Los Angeles at last issued formal apologies for historic actions of the Roman Catholic Church, as well as their personal actions, that had hurt or alienated groups and individuals. When an institution that affects many people has acted in ways that damage others, the wounds on both sides are deep and lasting. A public apology is not a cure, but it is nevertheless a great and historic act. It can allow people to get past their pain and begin healing.

Robbing people of their specific group identity and their dignity can also inflict wounds. While we are all humans and we aim for a love of all humanity, it is crucial to the development of the ego that we be allowed to express our group identity. Ethnicity and religion are two examples of identity markers in modern society. Sometimes geography provides a major marker—"I'm a Texan" or "I'm a New Yorker." Lineage can be significant too: "My grandfather was a rabbi" or "I come from a long line of pastors." In some societies, gender provides a major marker, when for example men and women are initiated into very different roles. Even separatist identities, like being a gang member or participating in a political movement, may provide an important foundation, especially in late adolescence. Even though we know these are ultimately not spiritual in content, we must recognize that they are important as part of a developmental stage.

When an individual or a group has difficulty growing beyond that stage, a natural response is to lash out at someone who can be blamed. If solutions are not readily available to remedy past injustice, an individual or a group can create an entire ideology around its past oppression. It limits the opportunities for healing and perpetuates the wounds. What is the solution? Once, when discussing the difficulties of the Palestinian Arabs in Israel, I asked a rabbi his opinion of what was happening. Clearly, I said, the Palestinians have suffered a great humiliation both in the wars with Israel and in their frustrations since. What is the remedy for this? He answered simply, "Pride in accomplishment."

We have seen this approach in many situations. Mahatma Gandhi was known for his programs of nonviolent resistance to British oppression in India and South Africa in the first half of the twentieth century. What is not often remembered is that Gandhi insisted that a crucial part of the effort was self-help programs—people spinning their own wool and wearing homemade cloth—to build self-esteem. Without this, he believed, the people could not be strong enough to practice nonviolence.

Spiritual practice has been proven to be part of such efforts as well. Dr. Martin Luther King Jr. accomplished work similar to Gandhi in emphasizing "strength to love" rather than reaction against the dominant society. He drew on the spiritual riches of African-American Christianity, including a spirit of deep faith and willingness to forgive, to create a nonviolent movement that would begin to heal the wounds of racism. In parallel ways, Nelson Mandela and Archbishop Desmond Tutu led a peaceful revolution in South Africa, after Mandela's years in jail under the apartheid system, and they created what has been called a "politics of reconciliation."

The same strategies can work against our own demons. We can model, each in our own ways, taking full responsibility for our lives and refusing to be victims or to justify our lives by appealing to our pain. We can dip into the resources of our spiritual traditions to find the ways to broaden our perspectives, to forgive, heal, and reconcile. Finally, we must all become aware of the damage we have done by using our unique, separate identities as an excuse for separatism. Indeed, one of the motivations for this book came from my deep feeling that within my own tradition, Judaism, and in the relationship of Judaism to other religions, many wounds need to be healed. We must all develop a perspective on life that has its source in ultimate oneness. The *sefirot* of Perseverance and Surrender can help balance our collective world as well.

7

REALIZING YOUR INTENT

Each life converges to some centre
Expressed or still;
Exists in every human nature
A goal,

Admitted scarcely to itself, it may be,
Too fair
For credibility's temerity
To dare.

Adored with caution, as a brittle heaven,
To reach
Were hopeless as the rainbow's raiment
To touch,

Yet persevered toward, surer for the distance;
How high
Unto the saints' slow diligence
The sky!

Ungained, it may be, by a life's low venture,
But then,
Eternity enables the endeavoring
Again.

—EMILY DICKINSON, "THE GOAL"

SPIRITUAL AWAKENING

THE ENERGY OF THE NEXT *SEFIRAH* on the Path of Remembering, *Tiferet*-Splendor, is always calling to us. It is our purpose in life, our personal connection to divine vision. But we spend many years—at least twenty, and often twice that long—just growing up and establishing ourselves in life. Most people are not ready to answer the call of Splendor until sometime in early to middle adulthood, and many of us not until we are elders. We first have to go through the phase of becoming socially responsible individuals, contributing to society, caring for our loved ones, raising a new generation. In this process, we learn to support others emotionally and receive love in return. We learn what enriches us and what drains us. We have confronted problems and solved some of them. We have created the basic structures of "normal" human life.

Usually by this time we also have some sense of where our personal configuration emerged. We may be able to see our place in the dynamics of our family of origin, how we have left it behind or how we are still enmeshed in it. We can observe our stumbling blocks in social relations—"I'm too shy" or "I get too aggressive in arguments." We have a sense of ourselves, although we sometimes hamper ourselves with criticism. We are beginning at least to steer our emotional course through the pitfalls that everyone encounters, whether it be financial issues, the death of loved ones, career choices, or the joy and struggle of raising children. Hopefully, we are also able to see something of our society's place in history. At the end of the last chapter, we saw that it is possible to take responsibility in such a way that we allow the wounds that society creates to begin to be healed. We can even view ourselves as part of a larger "family" and see how we have been enmeshed in the limited perspectives of our society—and how we can transcend them.

All this means that we have begun to master the four lowest *sefirot*. Yet we still may not be clear about our appropriate role in the larger cosmic drama. If we are turkeys under the table, we can now stick our heads out from under the tablecloth and see that there's a bigger picture. But our appetites and insecurities often make us quickly go back under again. Especially in Western society, our basic physical needs have been amplified so that, despite all our labor-saving and time-saving devices, we still spend an enormous amount of time satisfying our needs. We're also greatly concerned about the opinions of other turkeys, so we are subject to social pressure as well.

A spiritual awakening can begin when we recognize the futility of the life of a turkey under the table. Even if we are not able to articulate the problem clearly, we see that many of the ways we spend our time, many of our daily activities, are simply different ways of doing the same old thing—providing ourselves and our families with food, safety, continuity, and some pleasure. We see that our lives are not so much different from others around us, or even from animals who do the same things on instinctive programming. Then we ask, "Is this all that human life is about? What does it matter if I do this or not—billions of others live such lives. I'm trying to be a good person and manage what I've been given to manage. But what for? Why am I here?"

These questions arise out of a higher level of our being than our emotional and social selves. They represent an igniting of the spark of the soul, coming through the *sefirah* of *Tiferet*-Splendor, whose energy radiates from the center of our being. Once the energy of this *sefirah* is awakened, we have to listen to it. If we try to shut it off or ignore it, we will damage ourselves and short-circuit the higher development of our lives. Our questions have to do with our inner truth—indeed, Truth is another word for this *sefirah*.

As the great first-century Rabbi Hillel said, "If I am not for myself, who will be?" Society, however much it supports our development, will always set limits on personal development because social institutions necessitate certain demands for conformity. Even our friends and spouses may feel uncomfortable if we change too much because we may rock the boat. The *sefirah* of *Tiferet*-Splendor, which now begins to shine with divine light, insists that we go on a personal search.

We look upward now, not backward to our past or horizontally to our current companions who are in our emotional and spiritual comfort zone. Imagine that the four lower *sefirot* form a goblet, looking upward to be filled by the reality of our awakened soul.

Our search can take many forms. Frequently, it involves turning to religious or spiritual teachers or organizations. This is quite appropriate because they are the bearers of the deepest wisdom of spiritual seekers of all the ages. Although we may intuit that the truth lies within us, we are usually not so arrogant as to think that we can answer all the deep and important questions without listening to the voices of those who have preceded us. Every accomplished spiritual person has spent time learning from the elders, from people in their own tradition, or other traditions, who give over their wisdom.

At the beginning, you may find your teacher by going to the religious group of your choice and meeting all the "experts" (priests, ministers, rabbis, and so on). Frequently, the person you choose turns out to be simply the person who introduces you to the workings of the tradition. He or she is a gatekeeper. As you move on, the teachers you need will often appear in a more indirect way and may not even be professionals. Sometimes they will be in your life for a long time, sometimes for only brief encounters. It is almost as if they can't be consciously sought. As the old saying goes, "When the student is ready, the teacher will appear."

Most of us receive great benefit from attaching ourselves, for a time, to a specific teacher who not only imparts knowledge but is also a model of action, someone to emulate in many ways. Learning happens at a much deeper level when we see another person living the teaching.

Yet a relationship with a spiritual teacher has its dangers. The intense personal relationship to a teacher is a little like being put in a parent–child relationship again. Precisely because of its intensity, the relationship often awakens early emotional attachments and wounds. As a result, we can sometimes be blinded by the wonderful things that happen in the relationship, to the point that we forget the original purpose—to find our own truth. We can be dragged back into the emotional dynamics of the lower *sefirot*, and until we untangle them, we move forward only very slowly. Remember that the teacher is only a channel, the one you happen to have at this particular time. Review meetings with your teachers and fellow students on an ongoing basis to release the emotional energy that you sometimes attach to them.

CREATING A PRACTICE

Most important, a good teacher will introduce you to a practice. The practice guarantees that ultimately you will not be a mere imitation of your teacher. The practice will also be something that has been passed down in an authentic tradition. The various traditions usually suggest methods of self-examination and self-transformation: charitable acts, physical discipline, prayer, confession, meditation, ritual, and ceremony. We will look briefly at these approaches.

First, however, it is important to note that spiritual practice is not on the same level as rules. We talked about rules and roles as part of the *sefirah* of *Malkhut*-Manifestation, part of being in society. For example, your religion may have as one of its rules that you should donate one-tenth of your income to charity. However, taking on charity as a spiritual practice is a different matter. You are being asked to become a person who *embodies* justice and compassion and giving, rather than just obediently following a rule. Similarly, you may have grown up with certain traditional prayers or the ritual of confession. Now, however, you are asked to *become* your prayer and to continually examine how you are practicing your spiritual values. In truth, the rules of a spiritual tradition are intended to be part of a practice. If you grew up with them, you probably will see them as merely rules. If you come to them later in life, it may be clearer that they point to a spiritual practice. Either way you will, at this stage, revolutionize all your ideas about rules.

In Judaism, the path of Jewish law, known as *halacha,* is intended to refine the human being. The word that means "to refine" (*tzaref,* as in removing impurities) can also mean "to join," as when a metal worker joins two pieces with a soldering iron. When we have a practice, we begin the process of refining our human selves and joining ourselves firmly to God. The study of different religious traditions reveals that most of them offer similar recommendations as to how to improve your spiritual life. They all teach a moral framework for life, the discipline of your emotions, the improvement of your mind, maintaining the health of the body, and self-examination as you proceed on the path. These are all the work of the *sefirah* of Splendor.

The practices I describe below are, in my view, virtually universal, although the forms they take are unique to each religion. Look in your own Christian tradition for practices that fall into these categories.

1. *Study and reflection*

Since you're reading this book, this form of practice is probably an easy one for you. Go to lectures or classes by people who aim to challenge and not merely excite their audiences. Study the foundational religious texts—in the Jewish tradition, there is a truly outstanding and fascinating tradition of Torah study. Find out who are considered truly great deep thinkers and inspiring personalities in your tradition. Even if you can tackle only small pieces of their writings, remember that mastering a paragraph or a few pages written by a real thinker is worth far more than secondhand information. You can join the inquiry into the great questions that have occupied human beings for millennia: How can we understand the goal of human life? How do we make decisions in a way that promotes goodness? What is the origin of evil and how do we address it in our lives? Some people will be drawn more to this type of study than others, but it can be at least one component of everyone's spiritual path.

At the same time, if we acquire knowledge but it remains external to us, spiritual growth will not take place. Expertise in theology, philosophy, or religious law, if taken alone, can be just another "trade skill." It can be treated as a mere database of objective knowledge that we trot out on demand, but don't think much about in between. Religious knowledge must be internalized. A teacher who helps us understand our studies is essential here. The word *Kabbalah* means "receive," because the tradition had to be received personally, by one person from another, in direct transmission. This was indeed the method of the entire Jewish tradition: God taught Moses, Moses taught Joshua, Joshua taught the Israelite elders, and so on. The written tradition, inscribed in stone or scrolls or books, was the starting place, but not the whole of learning. A teacher or group studying together can help each of us internalize what we learn and apply it to our lives.

Two other practices work in tandem with study to help us incorporate the concepts and information we learn. These are prayer and meditation.

2. Prayer

Prayer is both a ceremony and a personal address to God. Ideally, in prayer we create our own sacred space, closing off the outside world, and speak from the core of our being to the power that guides the universe. Many prayer traditions follow specific forms that help us move toward that inner core.

Our personal address to God involves at least two dimensions. One is simply to become comfortable in talking to God. We can even speak aloud from our hearts about our own needs and problems—our personal needs, family or business problems, ideals, and goals. This approach is such a natural way to relate to divinity that it is found in every spiritual tradition.

Another good exercise is to make up your own prayers after learning a specific subject matter in your studies. Rabbi Noson of Nemirov, the chief disciple of Rabbi Nachman, composed prayers after each teaching he received from his master. This enabled him to internalize the teachings more fully. In kabbalistic terms, this is using the energy of the *sefirah Da'at*-Knowledge to "bind" one's mind to the subject at hand. For example, you might compose a prayer about the use of visualization, perhaps along the following lines: *May it be your will, God, that my imagination be turned to holy things, and that I be able to visualize and internalize the deep and profound concepts I am trying to learn.*

The second dimension of prayer is to focus less on ourselves and more on others. Prayer for the larger collective is instilled in Jewish prayers by the fact that most traditional prayers are worded for "us," the entire Jewish people. Some prayers are even broader in concept, extending to the entire human race. Think of yourself as an agent appointed to speak to God on behalf of others.

Biblical commentators have discovered hints about the importance of this aspect of prayer in the second chapter of Genesis, which tells the story of the first couple, Adam and Eve. It says that "no rain had yet watered the earth" (Gen. 2:5). Yet, we just learned in the first chapter that all the components of nature had been created, including vegetation and trees. How could this be? It is explained that all the vegetation existed *in potentia,* beneath the surface of the earth, but it had to wait for the rain to come before it could actually sprout. What caused it to sprout? The prayers of Adam and Eve![1]

Prayer demands that we go beyond ego. At the same time, prayer is an emotional experience—not a physical experience like giving money, nor an intellectual experience like study. One of the great contributions of Hasidism to Jewish practice was a renewed emphasis on prayer and on putting one's heart into prayer. When we try to speak from the depths of our hearts, we discover the deep pain and the profound joy of human existence, both our own and the pain and joy we feel on behalf of others. This is one of the emphases of the Hasidic masters—to cry from the depths of our hearts. As Heschel wrote, "I pray because God, the *Shekhinah,* is an outcast. I pray because God is in exile, because we all conspire to blur all signs of His presence in the present or in the past. I pray because I refuse to despair."[2]

Many people still ask, "What does our personal prayer have to do with the plans of the master of the universe? Does our prayer change God's design? Aren't people really praying just to satisfy their own emotional needs?" Remarkably, scientific studies suggest that prayer is healing, and particularly that prayer for others is effective. Generalized prayer for "the best outcome" or "thy will be done" seems to be especially effective, both on those who are praying and on those who are prayed for.[3] Exactly how prayer works is not understood, but these studies suggest we should not be so surprised that every religious tradition in the world has some way of invoking and asking the higher powers for protection and assistance.

3. Meditation

Meditation in Judaism is a complement to prayer. To put it colloquially, if prayer "goes up," meditation prepares us to receive what "comes down." Thus an important aspect of meditation is to inculcate awareness and receptivity. Another dimension is contemplation, including visualization, which helps us engage our imagination and feeling so that our connection to the Divine can become richer and more complete.

Kabbalistic meditations have ranged from simple *kavannot*—reciting or thinking an "intention" for a specific prayer—to intricate and complex transmutations of the letters of divine names. Silent meditation and breathing exercises were quite common among kabbalists just as among Hindu and Buddhist teachers. Such methods of increasing awareness, on the one hand, and ability to concentrate and focus, on the other, seem to be nearly universal. Most practitioners of such methods also testify that they help in achieving equanimity, a peaceful and serene attitude in the face of life's difficulties.

The first stage of many Jewish meditation practices is called "settling the mind."[4] This settling of one's *Da'at,* or Knowledge, becomes a platform for the utter holiness of the upper levels. In addition, Jewish tradition teaches a specific kind of meditation that can sometimes enable us to be receptive to what is beyond the boundaries of normal thought: *hitbonenut* (from the same root as *Binah-*Understanding). Literally it means "to cause oneself to understand." This approach involves focusing on a particular symbol or concept and connecting it mentally to related symbols and ideas. A *hitbonenut* meditation on water, for example, might involve contemplating water in the various forms it appears on earth, water as a symbol for Torah, verses in the Bible that mention water, and the Hebrew word for water (*mayim*) and the meanings of its letters. All these would be "unfoldings," so to speak, of the symbol water.

Meditative visualizations have long been recognized in Kabbalah as a powerful aid to spiritual understanding. Rabbi Noson of Nemirov wrote that imagination can be thought of as the highest point of the physical realm and the lowest point of the spiritual realm.[5] In meditative visualization, we use verbal cues to imagine a certain feature of existence—for example, resting in the presence of God in the Garden of Eden. We do this almost instinctively when we say, "Imagine yourself in the other person's shoes"—essentially a visualization intended to evoke compassion. The number of possible meditative visualizations is limited only by one's imagination. For millennia, the Book of Psalms in the Bible has provided rich subjects for contemplation. In Orthodox Christianity, icons have been an object of meditation. Stories of Jesus, saints, or holy individuals provide a nonvisual but mentally vivid focus for contemplation.

4. *Rituals and ceremonies*
Every spiritual tradition has a round of rituals, including daily and weekly rituals, ceremonies connected with lunar or solar calendars, and rites of passage. These rituals are often rooted in ancient spiritual practices and are maintained simply as traditions. Reforming movements in modern religion often throw them out (for example, many Protestant traditions vis-à-vis Roman Catholicism, Reform Judaism vis-à-vis the received Orthodoxy). A few generations later, however, they creep back in. Humans need to connect with natural rhythms, with a sense of heritage, and with their own bodies in a sacred way. Rituals enable us to do this.

There is an even deeper dimension to ritual. Recall that in speaking of *Binah,* I said that the patterns or templates of a tradition are laid down mentally in that *sefirah.* Rituals give these patterns physical, bodily form. They are the architecture of energy. They are rich in metaphor, symbol, and allusion because metaphor is the link between ideas (in the mind, in Understanding) and the physical and emotional (in the body, in Perseverance and Surrender).

Take, for example, rituals using trees or symbols of trees, which occur in many traditions. Judaism's menorah (the candelabra used in celebration of Hanukkah) is the image of a tree, the Tree of Life is a metaphor for the Torah, and, as we have seen, the kabbalists elaborated the structure of a tree to explain the entire cosmos. A procession with a Torah scroll embodies the process of bringing the Tree of Life and the hidden divine light into the world. The Christmas tree, originally from ancient European rituals, is decorated with ornaments suggesting rich fruits as well as illumination. These sacred trees suggest life, growth, a connection between earth and heaven, and branches extending out to the world and bearing fruit.

Every ritual has its repertoire of metaphors that connect us to untold depths within ourselves, enabling us to embrace the collective reality of humanity. Many of Judaism's *mitzvot* (commandments) are rituals in that they provide physical connections with the basic template— for example, holiday rituals and symbols such as placing on the doorpost a *mezuzzah* (a case containing certain verses from Torah written on parchment) or wearing *tefillin* (phylacteries, leather boxes also containing verses, placed on the head and arm) during prayer. Many of these fall into the category of physical actions known as "witnesses," asking us to perceive in our bodies and in the physical world our connection to God. Christian use of the cross or crucifix provides a visible and tangible ritual image, and the cycle of the liturgical year vividly connects people with the life of Jesus, allowing Christians to perform an *imitatio Christi* through the seasons.

In connection with ritual, forms of music and dance should be mentioned. Although these may not be an essential part of every spiritual practice, many traditions include rhythm, chant, melody, and dance as part of ritual and liturgy. In Judaism, music is regarded as a delicately nuanced form that not only expresses heights of spiritual experience for some people, but also can aid in healing and in expanding consciousness, which can then lead people further on their search for connection with God. The vibrations of music enter the body in a way that is different from intellectual insights. Similarly, hymnody in Christianity, from Gregorian chants to modern evangelical music, has accompanied many important spiritual movements.

5. *Confession*

The practice of confession is connected to prayer, and also frequently to traditional rituals, but it deserves special mention on its own. It is amazing how long we can go without noticing our mistakes or, even when we do notice them, without truly acknowledging them. At the other extreme, some people are so hard on themselves that they seem to be constantly apologizing, believing that they are the cause of what goes wrong around them.

Many traditions have, therefore, ritualized confession, putting it in a set framework at certain times so that it is sure to get done, but also so that it will not become an unhealthy preoccupation. Judaism focuses on Yom Kippur, the Day of Atonement, which occurs each year in the fall. During the ten days before (and many people start preparing a month earlier), we are supposed to review our lives, make amends for what we have done wrong and not corrected, and confess our sins to God. Yom Kippur is the holiest day of the Jewish calendar because of the intense purification that is accomplished through such confessions, prayers, and fasting. Some Jews take on practices of self-examination and confession throughout the year—for example, the day before the new moon of each month, or on Friday afternoons before Shabbat.

In most other traditions some form of self-examination occurs, along with confession or discussion of problems with a more experienced person. In Roman Catholicism, for example, confessing serious sins to a priest is required before partaking of the Eucharist, as well as an annual confession during the Easter season. (Formerly known as penance, this rite is now called the sacrament of reconciliation.) In some traditions, confession may be much less formal. Protestants rejected the necessity of confession to a priest, but the American Puritans had long discussions with their ministers to help them assess their spiritual state. Methodists originally used group meetings as a way of sharing problems and clearing up issues, while encouraging one another in the faith. In modern times, twelve-step meetings (Alcoholics Anonymous and similar programs) have a practice of "taking inventory," which is then shared with a more experienced member. In monastic traditions as well as in Jewish *yeshivot* (seminaries), conversations with a spiritual director serve a similar purpose.

I mention these examples to indicate how pervasive the idea is, even if it is not called confession, of taking a good hard look at yourself and then speaking about it to another person and/or to God. The speaking is important. And the other person has the responsibility of responding truthfully and with deep respect and kindness to help you on your path—that is why it has often been a spiritual elder who takes this role. Of course the main point is fine-tuning, not browbeating, yourself. Clear sight is the aim, while accepting that each of us is imperfect.

6. *Charity (in Judaism,* tzedaka*)*

Every tradition teaches that people who have not renounced possessions altogether must practice charity, giving a portion of their possessions to those who have less, or supporting efforts to improve the physical or spiritual condition of others. The point of this practice on a spiritual level is to teach us to give more and more of ourselves, so that we recognize that our life is not ours. As the nineteenth-century scholar Samson Raphael Hirsch wrote: "You have nothing so long as you have it only for yourself, ... you only possess something when you share it with others. When you have experienced the supreme happiness of giving, then will you rejoice in the great task for which God has called you—to be a blessing."[6]

The two main forms of charity are connected to the *sefirot* directly above Splendor, namely Expansiveness and Restraint. When we act with Expansiveness flowing through us, we are giving and supporting others. When we act from Restraint, we are practicing noninjury to others and to our environment. Both these activities may involve an element of self-sacrifice. Indeed, charity is a natural form of sacrifice—a giving up of things to which the ego might attach itself.

There are three main aspects of acting from *Chesed*-Expansiveness, the outflowing of ourselves toward others. Each takes a multitude of forms in the unique configurations of our lives: the physical gifts we give to support others, the emotional gifts of caring for others, and the mental gifts of teaching others. The physical realm starts with the most elemental, such as giving life through becoming a parent, and feeding or providing food, clothing, and shelter for children or others who cannot support themselves. It includes caring for plants and animals, whether in our homes or in the larger environment. Healing people (or plants or animals) in the realm of the physical is part of this gift as well. Also, we may provide financial help for those who are accomplishing something for the general good that we cannot do ourselves—this is another aspect of the concept of charity.

Emotional giving means being available to others, giving the gift of your time and a sensitive heart. It also means sharing your feelings so that the sensitivity of others can be naturally awakened. This giving can be at home or in a profession, or simply in the social contexts of which you are normally a part. Even the simple gift of companionship can be an important contribution to someone else's life. In many cases, as in caring for children or in the healing professions, emotional giving overlaps with the physical, but it has its own distinctive value.

Mental giving means sharing your thoughts—not simply the words that fly out of your mouth, but your considered thoughts. When you contribute your thoughts to the world, you are a teacher. Your perspective is unique and valuable. Also, by treating others as your teachers, you will encourage them to develop their thoughts.

The other side of charity is noninjury, which is connected to the *sefirah* of *Gevurah*-Restraint. In some traditions, such as Jainism (an ancient religion of India), this practice involves a great effort to avoid harming even insects. In most traditions, more moderate versions of this idea appear. "Whatever is hateful to you, do not do to others" is the way the first-century Rabbi Hillel formulated this principle in Judaism. "Do unto others as you would have others do unto you" is the Christian scriptural version. Jewish law also includes injunctions not to cause anguish to humans or animals, not to destroy fruit-bearing trees, and not to waste things. In a sense, all the "negative precepts"—that is, prohibitions—are means of restraining the ego so as not to do injury to the world.

All these practices are comprised in the spiritual gift each of us gives to the world, through being an example. When you are a positive example to others, you are living as close as you can to your soul. This is expressed in a well-known prayer, adapted from St. Francis of Assisi:

> God, make me an instrument of Your peace.
> Where there is hatred, let me sow love.

Where there is injury, pardon.
Where there is doubt, faith.
Where there is despair, hope.
Where there is darkness, light.
Where there is sadness, joy.
Master of the Universe, grant that I may seek not so much
To be consoled as to console,
To be understood as to understand,
To be loved as to love.

7. Physical discipline
In earlier times, physical discipline usually meant ascetic practices such as voluntary fasting and often, in non-Jewish traditions, celibacy for part or all of one's adult life. Today, it may mean regular, conscious exercise. Disciplining the body is part of heightening one's awareness.

The enormous complexity of the human being and the variety of stimulants available in modern Western culture result in situations where our bodies are doing things they were not designed to do. We sit a great deal, we are "in our heads," thinking, planning, and talking to ourselves an enormous amount of the time, and we have easy access to an array of food and drink—not to mention drugs and cigarettes—that can throw our bodies off balance. When we try to impose a discipline, we usually have weak support systems (in contrast, say, to monks in a monastery). We bounce back and forth between being lax and overdoing our strictness. The great sage Maimonides, himself a physician, advised moderation in everything, but always living with attention to the health of the body.

Many spiritual practices include a body discipline, such as yoga or *t'ai ch'i*. Although the Jewish prophets of ancient times apparently used physical postures in their efforts to attain prophetic insight,[7] Kabbalah did not develop a distinctive or universal practice. Rabbis concerned about health advocated ordinary physical exercise like walking for people who were too sedentary—which includes quite a few of us today! From this, one can conclude that any healthful and invigorating practice, together with discipline around food and sexuality, is appropriate for most people.

8. Community

Last but not least is the practice of being an active supporter of a community. For people blazing their own unique paths, or for those who tend to think globally, this is not always easy. But our responsibility does not end with our own small circles of fellow travelers; it also requires us to contribute to a larger community. Judaism has always been rooted in the concept of a "people" and the concrete reality of a community, meaning either a synagogue or a neighborhood. At the very least, we must remember that our acts reflect, like mirrors, our larger community, either enhancing or detracting from it. We are always representing more than ourselves, and building up others as we grow. This is true at the level of family, community, and general religious identity. Community consciousness needs to be part of our spiritual practice. The Rabbis taught:"Do not separate yourself from the community" (*Avot* 4:5).

BEING WHOLEHEARTED

Although practice is essential, we can sometimes fool ourselves into thinking that the practice *is* our spirituality. Practice is just that: practice. All experts—the pianist, the runner, the welder—practice to acquire the skills that enable them to become masters. We practice our spiritual skills to master the art of godliness. Masters are those who perform their arts with complete integrity and involvement of self and with whole-heartedness. The same is true with religious practice.

The aim is expressed in a biblical phrase: "Be whole-hearted with the Lord your God" (Deut. 18:13). The goal is to become completely at one with our deepest self and with the infinite source. If we think that merely doing the practice is the same thing as being that self united with the source, we will end up in great confusion. The medieval philosopher Maimonides wrote that most of the commandments of Jewish law, which are largely prescriptions for *doing,* have *being* as their aim—the kind of being that is a channel for the Divine.[8]

For example, some people become very involved in the charitable works of their church, synagogue, or community organization and see this involvement as their spiritual practice. In reality, such work can serve two important functions: first, it supports the organization; second, it is a discipline in which individuals can practice lovingkindness. Both are quite appropriate. The first function is giving of our time in return for what we receive from the organization. This is primarily a form of social reciprocity, on the level of the *sefirot* of Perseverance and Surrender. It supports a good social institution of "companions," but it is not necessarily spiritual. The second function of such activities can be the real practice, namely, work on ourselves through the spiritual practice of charity, nourished by the *sefirah* of *Chesed*-Lovingkindness. If, when we practice charity, we become conscious of what happens to us and others whom we serve, if we literally "take it to heart" by being aware of our emotions, these actions begin to transform us. When we allow ourselves to feel and think about what we are doing, charitable activities help us become whole-heartedly involved in the divine design. The actions are no longer only about *doing* what is necessary to support a social structure, but also about *being* a different kind of person. The integration develops in the *sefirah* of *Tiferet*-Splendor.

The same can be said of any aspect of practice. Ritual can become empty form or it can be the architecture of divine energy. Obeying the rules can become an exercise in robotics or an act of deep love of God. Prayer can become habitual words or a flow from the heart, fired with *kavannah* (pure intent). Even meditation, which can lead toward a deep inward contentment, can become an occasion to fall asleep, literally or metaphorically. Our practice must be examined from time to time to see whether it is keeping us awake and awakening us to new levels or becoming a support of our ego, keeping us in our persona. What we want instead is that Splendor—our true inner being—shine through in Manifestation. We want our light to be revealed in our practice, so that the two are really one.

If we become attached to some area of practice, we need to look at what that attachment is about. Is it about ego, painting the right face for the outside world? Or is our fascination hinting at something deeper we need to learn about ourselves? If we love external rituals, perhaps it is because we need to develop our own sense of ceremony and the movements of energy. If we throw ourselves into charitable work, it may be because we need to develop our heart-connection with others. If we are attached to a teacher, perhaps that teacher mirrors the wisdom that is hidden within us. The key here is to become aware of what each discipline, each external thing we receive, touches within us. Every element of practice is also our teacher—and is the way we become our own teachers.

Thus, arriving at your true self does not mean that you no longer have to follow rules or do the activities of a practice. On the contrary, you will have found much more meaning in the rule, for you will have internalized it, making the practice your reality. A famous Zen story is told of a monk who, before he began practicing Zen, worked at the monastery, chopping wood and carrying water. Then he gave it all up to meditate until he reached enlightenment. What does he do now? He chops wood and carries water.

THE SOUL'S MISSION

As we take our spiritual life more seriously, we frequently find that we are being given more and more responsibility. For example, we may find that we simply must set aside more time for meditation and prayer—we just don't feel good if we try to skimp or rush through those activities. Or we may find that people are unexpectedly knocking on our door or calling us at odd hours for help or a sympathetic ear. Even if we thought we were partially retiring from our worldly busyness to commit to spirituality, we now have just as much business as before—but it's higher in quality, evoking more of our deeper selves.

These changes in our lives are signs that we are growing in spiritual status, being allowed to do more and more for God. As an analogy, think of an emissary sent out on particular missions. As he proves himself, he is given more and more difficult and exacting missions. He hones his skills, becomes more sure of himself, and eventually comes to the point where he can carry out the will of his superiors in very unusual situations, with an extraordinary degree of faithfulness to their intent.

Similarly, you have a mission on earth, which you are discovering. You are to fulfill the will of God by being here, with your particular talents that you bring to every situation—with your unique light to shine. You knew this when you came here. You forgot it in the womb. But you will eventually fulfill everything you were created for. One of my teachers calls this mission your "soul contract" with God. You and God worked this out before you came. You helped decide the contract's terms and conditions. You forgot—but now, when you are fulfilling them, you will know it.[9]

Think of times in your life where you felt "This is really me!" It may have been a brief moment of ecstasy when you accomplished a task or had a few moments to do exactly what you wanted. Or it may have been an extended time when you had really satisfying work, where you got up eagerly each day to do the job because it so suited you. Perhaps it was a time when you had a compassionate conversation with a friend who needed you, or when you were truly able to express yourself to someone else. Or a period of intense creativity when you simply forgot the world. Or a moment when you stood up to pressure and resisted the expectations of others, knowing that you had to be an example of integrity. You were, for that time, free of self-doubt, regret, or worry, free of demands other than your own inner motivation, and immediately present to whatever was at hand.

This sense of immediate presence is the reality of truth—your unique truth. In that moment, you were part of what is called the chariot of God, from Ezekiel's vision of the chariot (Ezek. 1); you were manifesting your divine image to the fullest extent you could at that point in time. You were connecting with oneness, not on the abstract level of thought or meditation or dream, but in full waking consciousness.

I have seen this wonderful event occur a few times in other people. I mentioned in the last chapter my acquaintances who survived the Holocaust as children in hiding. One was my husband, who for decades did not speak about the horrors of his childhood. Only in midlife, as more and more survivors were speaking out, did he begin to attend meetings and share his story with others. Yet he knew that he was telling it with a certain flatness, almost as if it had happened to someone else.

Years went by. Finally, in 1998, he decided to gather friends and relatives together to tell his story more fully. I was fortunate to be there, because it was one of those moments of truth. He had decided to tell the story not around suffering and horror, but around gratitude. With every detail, every excruciating event of running, hiding, escaping from the Gestapo, and more hiding, he had a tale of gratitude to tell. Not only gratitude to the non-Jews who hid him and his parents, but gratitude for every incident and every person who aided them in their journey, and gratitude to God.

The radiance of that evening was unforgettable. Often, the expression of our truth lasts only a moment for us—our "moment of glory," we sometimes say. But the event is no less radiant and powerful for its short existence in linear time.

As we develop spiritually, such moments can occur more often and last longer. Each time we experience a longer sense of our connection with God and our true purpose, it is as if a veil has lifted. As those veils part, one by one, the light of the true self shines through more and more clearly. Instead of appearing like a dusty old lamp, we wear our spiritual garments like a stained-glass window on a brilliant sunny day. On a social level, because we resonate with our own inner truth, we recognize that we are not merely a part of society, but that we also have a responsibility to create and give to society. We can contribute our own creative energies to the building of a better world in which to live. On the spiritual level, our connection to inner truth enables us to direct our prayers, our meditations, and our entire mental, emotional, and physical orientation toward a larger reality, beyond the personal self. Our moments of connection to the higher self and our divine source reveal that we are creative, loving, and giving in our very essence. What we want most of all is to express that fullness of being completely. In our deepest selves, we want to be completely true to our mission. We want to be responsible and responsive, from the very core of our being. Without this full responsibility, this quasi-divine responsibility, human life is no more meaningful than animal life. As Heschel wrote, "In order to be a man, a person must be more than a man."[10]

Look again at the Tree of Life. The *sefirah* of *Tiferet*-Splendor lies on a line coming directly from *Keter*-Crown, the arrow to the soul. Because of this connection, *Tiferet*-Splendor is a place of oneness, despite the dualities that pull it on either side. We can say that it is the place where we become conscious of truly being ourselves.

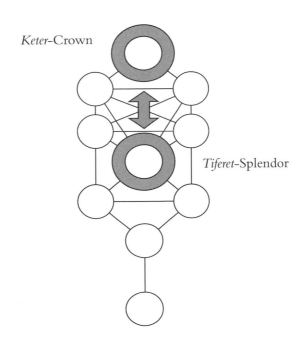

Keter-Crown

Tiferet-Splendor

8

REVEALING YOUR SOUL

The word stands for the body, but the symphony stands
for the spirit. All of Creation is a symphony.... which is
joy and jubilation.
—HILDEGARD OF BINGEN, *SYMPHONY OF THE HARMONY
OF CELESTIAL REVELATIONS*

THE LIGHT RADIATES FROM WITHIN

THE EFFORT OF PRACTICE opens new doorways. Our increasing willingness to take responsibility for purposeful living—the
work of *Tiferet*-Splendor—expands our horizons and gives us
new vision. Since we no longer see ourselves as victims of cir-
cumstance, we begin to understand that the experiences of
Gevurah-Restraint that used to seem like punishment are actually gifts. Since we are practicing becoming humble and
restraining our ego, we begin to recognize experiences of
Chesed-Expansiveness as great blessings, instead of brushing
them off as coincidences or taking credit for ourselves. This
refined perception of events will attune us more completely to
the movements of spirit in the world. Even though we still live
in a world of duality, we can function with less resistance and
more acceptance. Further, as we develop in prayer and meditation, we will find that work such as visualization, which evokes

fundamental spiritual patterns, enables us to enter the maternal matrix of *Binah*. As we learn to empty our minds and become more receptive, we may even recognize illuminations from *Chochmah*-Wisdom.

Traditionally, all these developments are portrayed as "ascents" to higher realms. However, as we will see more fully in this chapter, these changes can be better described in a different way. As we ascend by becoming more connected to our prayers, we will perceive our personal history—our "lower" life—in different tones. As we meditate more, we will become more compassionate to others and therefore will interact with them in new ways. As we refine each element of our character, our actions will become more in tune with our soul's true purpose. That in turn will enable us to enter into prayer and meditation with greater calm and purity of intent. Gradually, the light of the soul from "above" will illuminate the whole lamp, radiating from our faces with joy, from our hearts with love, and with both gentleness and power from our hands that touch, our mouths that speak, and our feet that take firm steps into the world.

What a promise! How can this happen? The deeper truth is that the fabric of consciousness, from the molecular level up to the Divine, responds to our purposive movement. When we make choices, our actions set up currents of events that eventually come back to us in one form or another. In Judaism, this is described as *midah k'neged midah,* like the English expression "measure for measure." As we exercise our powers with consciousness, the universe will respond and exercise its powers in return—at all levels, from the hard physical world of the soil we dig in our gardens to the plants and animals, from other human beings with whom we interact to spiritual entities and ultimately God. The late-twentieth-century physicist David Bohm put it quite clearly:

If we approach the world through enfolding its wholeness in our consciousness and thus act with love, the world, which enfolds our own being within itself, will respond in a corresponding way. This can obviously happen in the world of society. But even the world of nature will cease to respond with degeneration, due to pollution, destruction of forests, and so on, and will begin to act in a more orderly and favorable way.[1]

We can describe this spiritual development toward love and wholeness not as an ascent but as a spiral. We act from the heart, wholeheartedly, going with prayer and meditation "up" or "in" to the higher levels of consciousness, and moving with compassion "down" and "out" into the world, the lower realms of life. Unless we participate in both directions of movement, our spiritual growth will be stunted. We must become not only mystics, pursuing inward transformation, but also prophets, bringing the word of healing and transformation to the outside world as well.

We can begin to activate this spiral by recognizing angels.

A Chorus of Angels

Every event is a message from God. You may be riding in a subway, engrossed in your newspaper, when suddenly you notice the conversation of people next to you. A few minutes later, you are buried in the paper again. Why did your consciousness awaken at just that moment? Kabbalah says it was a message you were supposed to hear. Why? A warning from Restraint? A blessing that brings reassurance and comfort from Expansiveness? Your job is to decode the significance of the message in your life.

The word for messenger in Hebrew (*malach*) also means "angel." Angels are encounters with directed energy, sending us messages, often pulling us in a positive direction, sometimes warning us away from danger. I am going to use the word *angel* quite broadly to describe a variety of fairly common experiences that seem to be personal, energetic, and carrying information directly useful to us. We experience these energies around places, people, and the intangible dimensions of life. While this usage of the term may seem strange at first, it is in accord with the mystics' insistence that angels exist at every level of being. To use an analogy from modern physics, different angels exist on different frequencies. As we hear different kinds of music and conversation when we tune into different radio wavelengths, so angels "appear" to us in different ways.

Expansiveness is experienced as unconditional love, as blessing beyond our wildest dreams, as beauty and delight that take our breath away. Often those who write of experiences in nature express it best. The late-nineteenth-century naturalist John Muir wrote on one of his visits to the Sierra Nevada mountains:

> Here is calm so deep, grasses cease waving.... Wonderful how completely everything in wild nature fits into us, as if truly part and parent of us. The sun shines not on us but in us. The rivers flow not past, but through us, thrilling, tingling, vibrating every fiber and cell of the substance of our bodies, making them glide and sing. The trees wave and the flowers bloom in our bodies as well as our souls, and every bird song, wind song, and tremendous storm song of the rocks in the heart of the mountains is our song, our very own, and sings our love.

The Song of God, sounding on forever. So pure and sure and universal is the harmony, it matters not where we are, where we strike in on the wild lowland plains. We care not to go to the mountains, and on the mountains we care not to go to the plains. But as soon as we are absorbed in the harmony, plain, mountain, calm, storm, lilies and sequoias, forests and meads are only different strands of many-colored Light—are one in the sunbeam![2]

That sense of being "utterly at home," of being supported, cherished, and connected to the world around us, is the manifestation of Expansiveness. See this in your own life—think of times and places when you have felt surrounded by blessing—whether in the beauty of nature, in some activity, or among people who were special to you.

One kind of angelic experience occurs when we lose ourselves, when our felt sense of the boundaries between ourselves and the world dissolves. This is not an intellectual experience, where we detach from the world and go into our minds, but a place where we experience the world, or some aspect of it, so fully that it seems to carry us away. Sometimes this happens in nature, when we feel so much a part of everything around us that we are no longer conscious of being different from the scenery. Aesthetic experience can also bring this sense of disappearing: Hearing certain music exalts you, or you can wander through a museum exhibit so absorbed that time and space seem to dissolve. I still recall a Cézanne exhibit more than twenty years ago at the Museum of Modern Art in New York, where I stood transfixed before a series of studies by the great painter, each of the same scene, each slightly different. I got lost from my tour group and only after a long time, perhaps an hour in that one room, managed to tear myself away.

Such experiences are so overwhelming that we tend to speak of them as passive experiences: "I was drawn into the painting," "I felt uplifted by the music." At that moment, we have been touched and we give ourselves to the world as it has been offered to us just then and there. We feel supported and honored by the universe, and we actively embrace that givingness. This experience signifies that God has sent angels of *Chesed*-Expansiveness to carry us upward and envelop us, as if in a cloud of perfection, and we expand in return.

While some experiences are rare, like an encounter with great art, other angels come as regular and tangible sources of support in the form of things we love. The awesome isolation of the desert may delight one person, the intimacy of a forest stream may nourish another. You may prefer sitting quietly with a friend, while your neighbor may be drawn to the busy hum of downtown. These preferences have nothing to do with your talents—what you can *do*. Rather, these are forces that help you *be* the person you truly and deeply are. We could say that if you are a person who loves the desert, the angel of the desert comes to support you when you go there—not only when you travel there physically, but also when you go there in meditation or contemplation.

Still another kind of angel appears as a sense of protection from danger, as when popular religion speaks of guardian angels. I first became aware of angelic protection when I traveled across Arizona and New Mexico in midsummer, only to discover when I stopped for gasoline that I was a thread of rubber away from a blowout in the desert. The gas station attendant looked amazed and said, "You've got somebody traveling with you." Although at one level I was embarrassed at having paid so little attention to my car, when he said those words, I had goose bumps and recognized, in some deep part of myself, that he was right.

Each of these experiences points to higher realms where our souls are nourished, often on a regular and fairly predictable basis. It is important to ask yourself what aspects of your world—what kinds of places, activities, times of day—support and nourish you. Where do you connect with the angels that accompany you? It could be by the tree in your backyard or at your computer (is there an angel dancing on my monitor right now?), on your next airplane trip or at your place of worship, in intellectual work or when you participate in a sports event. When you choose to go to a place or enjoy an activity that feels like one of your pillars of support, think of it as a mirror of your soul's true love—and that God loves you through this experience.

Then there are aspects of experience that go beyond the angels of nature or angelic energies that infuse what is created by human hands. Here is where we find, in traditional contexts, the word *angels* used most often: an experience of the supernal comes with such force and clarity that angelic energy appears to take quasi-human form. Reports of such experiences occur almost universally in religious traditions, including Judaism. Going back to the Bible itself, we find that angels came to Abraham in the guise of travelers on the road; an angel was stationed at the gate of the Garden of Eden holding a sword; and a fearful angel stood in the path of Balaam and his donkey. Jacob wrestled with an angel, whom some commentators identify as the angel of Esau, his twin brother. Occasionally, prophets such as Ezekiel and Isaiah have seen in their visions angels that have unusual, nonhuman features—angels with wings or with many faces, angels in the shape of wheels with eyes, angels of fire.

Sometimes angelic energies actually coalesce around real humans. We experience a unique energy from someone, of love and guiding support. It's hard to tell whether such an unusual quality is coming from the person's natural personality, or from the nature of the relationship, or is something that transcends human interaction. But it is a special blessing to have such a friend, teacher, or support group. Once in a while, you will find a person or a group that continuously and unequivocally supports you and allows you to relax your boundaries and transcend your own ego.

My most dramatic personal experience of such a development came after I had been trying to write a novel (an interesting challenge for a scholarly person). The novel was in part about a group of people who chose new members according to the inner quality of their souls. After several months of fits and starts, I gave up writing the novel. Then, about a month later, I was introduced to a group of women who were studying their dreams and the inner qualities of their souls! I had, unknowingly, evoked my own retinue of angels. Such gifts are great blessings, all the more because they are surprises. And sometimes the angels we experience in human form are even more amazing than the purely "energetic" angels.

Another angelic experience can occur after the death of a loved one. The form of the deceased presents itself to deliver a message—as does an angel—usually to a beloved friend or relative still on earth. Often, people have told me of appearances of loved ones in dreams; sometimes they also appear in waking reality. One woman reported to me that after her sister's death, she went for a walk in the woods behind the house. "Suddenly I heard the sound of beautiful music and saw my sister's form, walking with some people I didn't recognize, right ahead of me. She was very happy." Personally, I was given the gift of knowing my mother was being accompanied by familiar angels—her own sisters—on her death journey. After the convalescent home called me to say that my mother had taken a turn for the worse, I drove there as quickly as I could. As I drove down the freeway, I unexpectedly saw, just above the hood of my car, the form of two of her older sisters whom my mother had loved dearly and who had passed away many years before. Such experiences tend to be stronger around the time of a death because, as many writers have observed, the veils between the lower and the higher realms become thinner at that time, so we can "see" the angels or the souls that come to support us.[3]

Yet such events do not always occur immediately after death. My husband was astounded to experience the presence of his deceased uncle, Max, in another way. Several years after Max died, my husband said the customary special prayers in synagogue on the anniversary of Max's death. Later that morning, he was cleaning out the garage and came across a box of old audiotapes, some of which were unidentified as to the contents. He popped one into the tape player to see what it was and immediately heard Max's voice. Max, it turned out, had recorded a greeting to my husband many years before, to send him blessings. The tape had, ever since, been lying among family possessions, waiting for that day when an angel could deliver the message from Max.

Angels and other souls do support us. An ancient Jewish text teaches that before every human being walks a retinue of angels, shouting, "Make way for the image of the Blessed Holy One!" Perhaps this is the most delightful group of angels. May we be blessed to see them each time we encounter another person.

LIFE'S CHALLENGES

Experiences of Expansiveness can provide us with such a high that sometimes we become frightened when the other side appears. Angels of Restraint are often guardians of the sacred, like the angel at the entrance to the Garden of Eden, and they remind us of where we cannot go. Others are challengers, like Esau's angel in a wrestling match with Jacob. In our ordinary life, we tend to think of these angels as the lessons we have to learn. Unlike the often painful lessons of lower levels, however, the angels of Restraint come as midcourse corrections or fine-tunings of our direction in life. By the time we reach the level where we are acting from the heart-space of *Tiferet*-Splendor, we are resonating with our core self most of the time. Here we know that even the "bad" things in life are methods to enhance our ability to accomplish our purpose in the world. Or, as the Reverend Dr. Martin Luther King Jr. put it, "We can never travel beyond the arms of the Divine."[4]

Sometimes Restraint is purely an inner experience. For example, we feel unsuccessful in efforts to accomplish tasks, or to reach out to people, and we begin to wonder whether our life really makes sense. We may be unable to pray, but at the same time we feel needy and anxious. We wonder if we are alone in the universe. The great Rabbi Joseph Soloveitchik, one of the most learned men in both Judaism and secular studies in the twentieth century, wrote of this side of experience in his book *Lonely Man of Faith*. Humanity, he believed, has two dimensions. One is what he called "majestic Adam," the side that leads us to master our environments and create the world. The other side is that of "lonely Adam," a side that feels untouched by our creative accomplishments and unfulfilled no matter how many loving and rewarding personal relationships we have.

The loneliness can be frightening, but when we recognize that it is merely a doorway to another dimension of relationship to God, we can walk through it. We are being asked to develop a very private and personal relationship to God. It is as though God is saying, "I am not always to be found in my vast creation. Come and meet me in secret." The messenger calling us to inwardness—like Isaac who "dug deeper" the wells of his father—comes from *Gevurah*-Restraint.

Sometimes, the angels of Restraint appear in external experiences, making our lives more difficult. Many of the world's great mystics and religious reformers have been persecuted or, at least, subject to great controversy. Even today, people on a spiritual path may still encounter opposition or skepticism. More commonly, Restraint appears in the form of great disappointment—for example, in a teacher or friend on whom one had counted—or a physical injury or illness that requires us to confront ourselves. The great spiritual teachers say that everyone on a spiritual path must encounter such challenges at one time or another, because they help us fight the potential for ego-inflation that comes with spiritual growth. As we can see from incidents in the lives of many modern gurus and religious leaders of all denominations, no one is exempt from such dangers.

Every expansion must meet a limitation, just as the lava from the erupting volcano eventually cools in the sea. Our spiritual expansion will be challenged as well. If we accept the challenge, we may encounter important teachings or individuals who can deepen our path. A minor way this happened to me was a shoulder injury that simply would not clear up on its own. After months of resistance to seeking help, I was led to a healer and movement therapist, and the ensuing effort led me to a much deeper connection with my body. People who experience illness or opposition often discover new friends and supporters to help them through their crisis.

When we are visited by the angels of Restraint, we often do best by retiring to our own private container. This can be a place of deep meditation, long walks alone, or soaking in a hot tub with nothing but our own thoughts. When we go on this path, we are defining ourselves by connecting to deeper layers of our unique being. We may feel withdrawn from the world, but close to God. What happens in this withdrawal, this personal contraction of our energy, is that we can become more in touch with our own unique ways of seeing and experiencing things. We learn to discriminate, giving attention to what is significant and reducing our involvement in the trivial. Most important, as we learn to hear the messages of angels, we gradually begin to trust God in a more profound way, for we realize that messages are being sent to us all the time.

We also develop a deeper level of what is called "conscience"—a word that was once an important ethical term, but has fallen by the wayside. Literally, it means "knowing together with"—a knowing that connects us to the largest realities we can conceive. When we turn to our conscience, we examine ourselves in the light of the highest values we have. We become introspective and discover our true orientation toward life. We create a personal ethic, frequently much more demanding than that of our culture. We become more careful to avoid doing harm to ourselves and others, physically, emotionally, and spiritually. We ask ourselves frequently, "Are we living impeccably—committed and consistent with what we know to be good and what we understand to be God's will?" Sincere, honest self-examination is an important tool for building our self-esteem.

When we develop this characteristic, we can live without fear of human judgment. *Gevurah*-Restraint is classically regarded as associated with severity and judgment. Too many times, however, we are not so much concerned about what God thinks of us as what humans think. If we know our own conscience, the fear of external judgment vanishes. On the other hand, our relationship with God also becomes clearer. A famous Hasidic story tells of a certain simple man named Zusya, who lived in poverty and devotion to God. When he was ill, shortly before he died, he cried and cried. His disciples asked him why. "Reb Zusya, you were as kind as Abraham! You were as devoted as Isaac! Surely you don't need to be afraid of judgment by God." Zusya replied, "God is not going to ask me, 'Why weren't you like Abraham? Why weren't you like Isaac?' He's going to ask, 'Why weren't you Zusya?'"

God says to each of us, "I created you in a unique and beautiful way to reflect the divine image. Where did you fall short of what you could have been?"

ACHIEVING EQUANIMITY

Chesed-Expansiveness is so fulfilling and supportive that it contains the possibility of grandiosity or ego-inflation. *Gevurah*-Restraint keeps this in check. It brings us back to humility, which is the only place from which spiritual growth can occur. When we accept as angelic gifts the restraints that are given to us, the result is equanimity.

Many spiritual traditions teach the importance of achieving this quality. *The Code of Jewish Law* begins with the phrase "I keep God before me always," which, the mystics say, can also be read as, "I make everything equal before God." Kabbalah teaches that if we are moved one way or the other by events or people, experiencing approval as pleasure and disapproval as pain, we are not yet ready for the advanced spiritual path. Here is a story of a mystical rabbi of the early centuries CE that exemplifies this teaching:

> A sage once came to one of the Meditators and asked that he be accepted into their society.
>
> The other replied, "My son, blessed are you to God. Your intentions are good. But tell me, have you attained equanimity or not?"
>
> The sage said, "Master, explain your words."
>
> The Meditator said, "If one man is praising you and another is insulting you, are the two equal in your eyes or not?" He replied, "No, my master, I have pleasure from those who praise me, and pain from those who degrade me. But I do not take revenge or bear a grudge." The other said, "Go in peace, my son.... You are not prepared for your thoughts to bound on high, that you should come and meditate. Go and increase the humbleness of your heart, and learn to treat everything equally."[5]

Equanimity can develop when we recognize that everything is from God, and we are simply the channel to receive and transform it. The Bible tells a story of King David, who was the object of much controversy and even hatred from his opponents, who considered him a usurper of Saul's throne. One day he was walking with some of his soldiers, and a man standing by the side of the road started cursing him. David's guard, indignant at the man's insults, offered to kill the man.

> But the king said, "What has this to do with you, sons of Zeruiah? If he curses and if the Lord has told him to curse

David, who can question it? ... Let him be, let him curse, for the Lord has told him to do it. But perhaps the Lord will mark my sufferings and bestow a blessing on me in place of the curse laid on me this day." (2 Sam. 16:10–13)

Retaliation for evil is not the answer, but rather faith in God. However, that is often easier said than done. As we experience the energies of Expansiveness and Restraint, we must learn to allow the pain and disappointment simply to *be* what they are. Eventually, we will discover that truly, everything is simply a lesson. With this equanimity comes humility. And humility means recognizing our authentic reality as channels of divinity in this world. Our central *sefirah* of *Tiferet*-Splendor is then infused with new inner strength.

RUNNING AND RETURNING

The spiritual path does not end with mere acceptance. Equanimity is the stable foundation for deeper, broader, higher explorations. A new level of yearning stirs in our hearts because, in the midst of great blessings and difficult trials, we long to express our gratitude and love to God. We find ourselves seeking to go beyond the flux of ordinary experience and beyond awareness of angelic forces, to connect with God, with our source, with the one. God becomes the beloved, the one we are seeking. Yet we find, always, that we are limited in our ability to be with God. We may begin to have experiences of closeness—in Hebrew called *devekut,* or "clinging" to God—but we also find ourselves often separate, feeling far from God.

In the great religious traditions, the themes of union with and separation from God recur often. The famous work by John of the Cross, "The Dark Night of the Soul," is one of many medieval works that pivots around the soul's longing for God. The Song of Songs in the Bible is one of the Jewish tradition's expression of this profound theme. Traditionally, this poem is understood as an allegory of God's relationship to Israel or, alternatively, God's relationship to humanity. In it we find expressed the awareness of separation:

> Where has your Beloved gone, O fairest of women?
>   Which way did your Beloved go, that we may help you seek him?

And of union:

> I am my Beloved's, and my Beloved is mine.

The mystics call this experience "running and returning."[6] We "run" toward the Divine, we "return" to our ordinary existence. The moments of "running" in mystical experience energize the higher *sefirot* of *Chochmah*-Wisdom and *Binah*-Understanding, taking us to levels of illumination and insight that transcend our personal existence. These levels are completely holistic, part of the world of unity, not divisible into individual entities. As we saw in Chapter 2, the Jewish sages said that the upper three *sefirot* are "completely loving-kindness," meaning that when we can experience them, we will know them as completely and unequivocally energies of unconditional divine love.

Such experiences are rare—but perhaps need not be as rare as we sometimes imagine. We may encounter energies of Understanding or Wisdom through dreams, meditation, or other altered states of consciousness. The illumination of Wisdom can come as an experience of light, of awareness, or of love. You might wake up one morning feeling completely and deeply at peace. The experience of Understanding usually has more specific content. For example you might find, while studying (using the energy of Da'at-Knowledge), that the meaning of one of the symbols of your religion becomes transparent, and you feel as if you understand it profoundly. Or you might have a special dream that stays with you, giving you a feeling of assurance, even though you do not yet understand it.

It is not easy to hold onto such experiences in ordinary waking life. This difficulty is what the mystics call the aspect of "returning." We often have difficulty remembering our dreams, and we frequently doubt the validity of the "transconscious" experiences we are aware of. As a result, we often do not believe that intuition or inspiration are "real," or that dreams, clairvoyance, or visionary consciousness really take us into upper realms. But, like the category of angelic experiences, which are helpful messages with an extraordinary quality, intuitive and visionary experiences are also real.

The mystical masters also tell us that these experiences have emotional correlates. We feel love and expansiveness in the phase of running. When we return, we feel our smallness and distance, the nothingness of our ego. In Judaism, these emotions are called love and awe; they correspond to the sides of Expansiveness and Restraint. The *Tanya* describes them as two wings of a bird, both of which are needed to fly upward, that is, to achieve closeness to God. In love, we can identify with God and long to connect with the Divine. In awe, we stand back at a distance, so to speak—sometimes, as Kierkegaard wrote, in "fear and trembling," for, as we saw earlier, God is sometimes a consuming fire.

These waves of experience are normal. One cannot remain close to God for long periods of time. Even great spiritual masters have times of closeness with God and times of apparent separation, feeling distant from God. We will sometimes feel in touch with revelation or inspiration, or have insight and profound acceptance of the lessons of life. At other times, we will feel as though we are just doing our best to live by the rules and manage our ordinary lives. God is always present, but the nature of existence is such that we are sometimes riding on God's shoulders, so to speak, and sometimes we are part of the axle that makes the wheels go round. We must conquer any feelings of discouragement that may arise. "Never give up!" said Rabbi Nachman. We may feel we are in front of a brick wall, but soon we will see it is just a doorway. When we are able to open it, new possibilities will appear.

Notice, however, that this description, typical of many explanations of running and returning, suggests that returning is something negative. I want to suggest a different viewpoint. Yes, the mystic yearns for God and feels adrift and alone when life goes along at a "normal" pace. But if he is attached to the idea that true spirituality is the phase of running, his spirituality is feeding his ego! What God wants of us is that we should yearn *just as much* to manifest godliness in our everyday life as we yearn to have profound illuminations. If we truly understand that God is present in everything everywhere, returning can be just as fulfilling as running.

THE SPIRAL OF LOVING CONSCIOUSNESS

The realization that running and returning are simply two directions, that one is not less valuable than the other, is crucial to our understanding of Kabbalah. In fact, we can only go "up" (running) by also going "down" (returning). We can deepen inwardly only if we are willing to go out of ourselves, reaching out toward others. We can study, pray, and meditate all we want, but such practices will inevitably become ego-centered if we do not also incorporate compassionate action into our lives. We cannot enter into the higher realms solely by exerting our personal will. Rather, we must be doing God's will. That is why every Jewish mystic is expected to be a practicing Jew, doing the *mitzvot* (commandments) of Torah. That is also why so many mystics have sacrificed themselves caring for the poor and sick, or have challenged the inhumane restrictions of their societies.

Some elements of practice point upward—prayer, study, and meditation to Knowledge, Understanding, and Wisdom. Other practices, like charity and caring for your health, bring energies of compassion and wisdom downward, through Perseverance, Surrender, Foundation, and Manifestation. Up or down, they are all *practice*. We do them because they are good and they are godly actions, with as little personal attachment and as much humility as possible. Once we awaken to this realization, a new movement begins among all these *sefirot*. Our ascent also contributes to the elevation of what is below, and our involvement with the energies of the lower *sefirot* awakens deeper yearnings for connection with the higher realms.

As we proceed, we eventually come to see that even the division between "upper" and "lower" is artificial, because all spiritual energies proceed from and return to the heart, our central core, the energy of *Tiferet*-Splendor manifesting in us. Remember, the *sefirah* of Splendor is the *sefirah* of divine-human incarnation. As the *Zohar* tells us, it is the bolt that holds everything together, from the highest of heavens to the lowest place on earth. The more we are unified with our practice, the more we find ourselves being transformed into channels for godliness.

Let me make this point as clear as possible by portraying it on the Tree of Life. The movement of compassionate connection, to God and to the world, is a spiral that moves up, around, and down through all the *sefirot*. Look closely at the diagram on the next page as we follow the flow of energy.

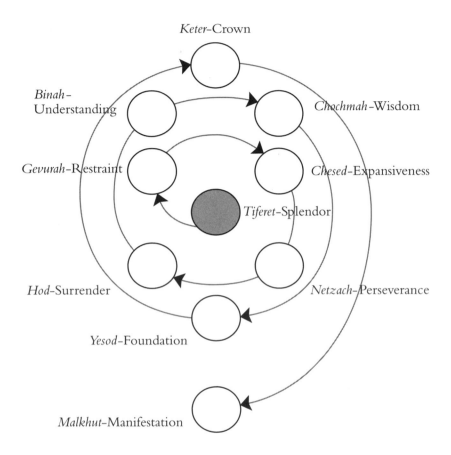

Keter–Crown

Binah–
Understanding

Chochmah–Wisdom

Gevurah–Restraint

Chesed–Expansiveness

Tiferet–Splendor

Hod–Surrender

Netzach–Perseverance

Yesod–Foundation

Malkhut–Manifestation

From the heart-center of Splendor, an arrow follows the energy to Restraint and Expansiveness. In our hearts we feel and perceive that we are continuously being directed and supported by Restraint and Expansiveness. This awareness changes our perception of our social environment, our friends, the way we spend our time, and the ways we experience our emotional life. These perceptions thus awaken new energies in the *sefirot* of Perseverance and Surrender, as the next arrow suggests.

As we perceive ourselves and our relationships differently, we begin to see more goodness in the world. This shift of consciousness connects to the upper *sefirot,* as the next arrow shows, because it involves an attempt to see the world through God's eyes. On each phase of creating the world, God said, "It is good." Thus Rabbi Kook wrote, "It is an art of great enlightenment ... to emulate the eye of God, that focuses only on the good."[7] We, too, want to see the goodness in the world, to see beyond the apparent differences and separations, and to remind ourselves that there is one loving God behind everything that manifests in the universe. This means connecting to Understanding and Wisdom.

With this new sight comes deeper insight from Understanding and Wisdom, enlarging our conception of the cosmos. We begin to recognize that the events and personalities familiar to us are only one small part of a grand design, one that has been unfolding for eons and involves, on this earth, billions of souls. From this perspective, our own story seems different. We can tell the story differently, we can pass on our heritage in a different and larger light—the insights from above affect our connection to Foundation. This is represented by the arrow from Understanding and Wisdom to Foundation.

Then, the stirring of the deep energies of creativity at Foundation spirals upward to Crown, following the next arrow. In some forms of yoga, the connection between these two energies is described as a physical experience (*kundalini*) in deep meditation. That it is sometimes described as the uncoiling of a snake parallels the idea of a spiral.

Even this highest energy spirals down again to Manifestation. Our deeds in the world then have the potential to be infused with the energy of the Divine. As light rays, as glistening raindrops, we have the ability to bring vitality to the world around us. As manifestations of divine soul, we can make life meaningful, vibrant, thrilling, joyous. Moreover, as we complete the circuit by acting in the world, the spiral of energy reverses, going up to Crown, which then energizes the whole again, returning finally back to the heart, filling it with more love and passion for God and goodness.

This redescription of the dynamics among the *sefirot* is very important. It reminds us that our creative energy spirals out from, and returns to, the heart, the place of Splendor, the divine image. We must not be tempted by the transcendence of blissful experiences of Understanding- or Wisdom-consciousness to forget our mission to the world. Nor should we trust too much even in Knowledge, our faculty for study and concentration, for a person can be extremely intelligent but hardhearted. Rabbi Dessler, a modern expert on personal ethical development, writes, "God chose ... the perceptions of the heart.... Intellect may fly high but only the heart can influence actions."[8] From the perspective of Kabbalah, the higher levels must be united with the lower, and this can happen only at the heart. *Tiferet*-Splendor is the place of passion for life and compassion for others, of love for God, for the divine purpose, and for all creation.

The connection that Kabbalah embodies between the upper and the lower worlds, between the higher reaches of spirit and the ordinary tasks of life, is no accident. In Judaism, mystical techniques were originally developed by the ancient prophets, who demanded of kings, priests, and rich men that they pay attention to what God wanted in the world—to care for the poor and relieve the suffering of the oppressed. Kabbalah, however visionary or esoteric it may have been, is rooted in a tradition of caring for the world. This intense sense of responsibility has sometimes faded into the background, but it is absolutely essential. One can only rise as high as one can bend down. If we are not involved in compassionate action on behalf of our families, communities, and societies, our ability to ascend will be limited. Conversely, if we do not have a spiritual practice that asks us to soar to the heights, we will be restricted by the natural forces of the social and physical worlds in what we can accomplish.

This is the true meaning of "running and returning." Running means going to God; returning means coming back not only to the self, but to discerning, caring involvement in the world. Returning means using our new vision to see anew, using our deeper sensitivity to feel compassionate.

THE GIFT OF THE SOUL

Spiritual growth, like physical growth, does not always go smoothly and evenly. Occasionally, we may find ourselves out of synchrony with parts of our life. Adults on a spiritual path often experience emotional roller coasters that we thought we had left behind with adolescence. For example, when we take on a religious practice, or return to one left behind long ago, our families may be bewildered. We may not feel so certain about what we are doing either. We say to ourselves, "Is it worth it? Maybe I should just forget about it." Or we pretend a certainty we don't really feel and go around preaching to our friends about how great our new practice is: "You should try meditating—it will help you straighten out your life." In truth, what is being called forth from us is greater compassion, a more heartfelt relation to the world.

Have faith that, as each issue in your life is brought into the light of a spiritual purpose, you will become more in tune with your own divine essence. It is almost certain that you will be called to go back and review the issues of your personal history to attune everything to a new level. For example, after I began a new level of spiritual work in a dream circle, I had a series of dreams that were very exciting because they seemed to hint at a true spiritual journey. Then I started dreaming about my parents, old friends, and what seemed to be familiar psychological issues. My dream teacher reassured me that I was not becoming more neurotic but just reintegrating my perception of my parents and childhood into a new picture of myself. Over time, I saw the same process recur with other dreamers and found in my own life that what she said was true.

We will eventually come to the place where we no longer feel compelled by the past or anxious about our path into the future. We will become confident—hopefully without arrogance—that we are on the way to manifesting our souls, being who we were meant to be. We don't suddenly become gurus or develop an amazing romantic relationship with our spouses. In fact, we frequently make no obvious external changes at all. Like the Zen priest, we chop wood and carry water. But we take responsibility by making conscious choices in the context of a wholehearted commitment to life: Today, here and now, we will continue polishing our lamps and allow the light of divinity to shine through us.

Usually, as we develop spiritually, we are given more choices to make and more responsibility to carry. This happens to almost every person who begins to demonstrate more trust, faith, and courage in the work of the soul. It is as if God's angels are monitoring our progress in cleaning our lamps of their sediment, and when our lights start to shine a little brighter, we are given more area to illuminate. Thus as we come closer to God, we move to a higher perspective on the mountain, so to speak. We see more work to do, and we feel greater responsibility for it. This shift doesn't necessarily make our lives easier. But the work becomes more interesting, exciting, and fulfilling.

This is the way we bring the gifts of our soul to earth. At the same time, we don't achieve this by directly willing it. The ultimate secret of heaven is that the gift of our soul appears without our conscious volition as we surrender more and more deeply, as we respond to whatever appears before us each day. As many spiritual teachers insist, the work of life is more about getting out of God's way than about doing what we think ought to be done. As Meister Eckhart wrote, "To the extent that you eliminate self from your activities, God comes into them.... People ought not to consider so much what they do as what they *are*; let them but *be* good and their ways and deeds will shine brightly."[9] This is the aim of a truly human life. We truly can aspire to become empty vessels, receiving the divine energy of our own souls and translating it into earthly reality. When the lamp is completely clear, radiant rainbow colors will shine through, and your deepest self will feel its harmony with divine purpose.

> Let our spirit fashion for us its creations. We recognize the angel, full of life, who attends to the act of birth, who brings into being his creations. He soars toward us from the great beyond, he draws close to us, he reveals himself in our souls. He has now come.
>
> —RABBI ABRAHAM ISAAC KOOK[10]

On the following page, for your review, are the *sefirot* as I described them in the Path of Remembering.

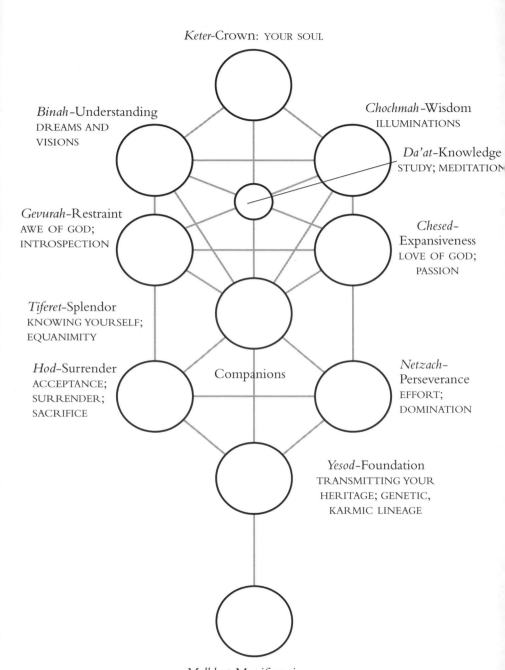

Keter-Crown: YOUR SOUL

Binah-Understanding
DREAMS AND
VISIONS

Chochmah-Wisdom
ILLUMINATIONS

Da'at-Knowledge
STUDY; MEDITATION

Gevurah-Restraint
AWE OF GOD;
INTROSPECTION

Chesed-
Expansiveness
LOVE OF GOD;
PASSION

Tiferet-Splendor
KNOWING YOURSELF;
EQUANIMITY

Hod-Surrender
ACCEPTANCE;
SURRENDER;
SACRIFICE

Companions

Netzach-
Perseverance
EFFORT;
DOMINATION

Yesod-Foundation
TRANSMITTING YOUR
HERITAGE; GENETIC,
KARMIC LINEAGE

Malkhut-Manifestation
NAMES AND ROLES; ACTION; MITZVOT

NOTES

INTRODUCTION: A NOTE ON THE HISTORY OF KABBALAH

1. See Neil Asher Silberman, *Heavenly Powers: Unraveling the Secret History of the Kabbalah* (New York: Grosset/Putnam, 1998), for a general history of Jewish mystical movements focusing on the culturally radical ideas those movements promulgated.

2. The best-known works by Luzzato translated into English are *Path of the Upright: Mesillat Yesharim* (Northvale, N.J.: Jason Aronson, 1995), *The Knowing Heart* (New York: Philip Feldheim, 1982), and *The Way of God: Pocketbook Edition* (New York: Philip Feldheim, 1999).

3. One example was Rabbi Samson Raphael Hirsch, who later became one of the outstanding Torah commentators of the nineteenth century and defender of tradition against Reform Judaism. Christian readers often enjoy his powerful book *The Nineteen Letters About Judaism,* trans. Karin Paritsky (New York: Philip Feldheim, 1996), for it sheds great light on the conflict between religion and modernity.

CHAPTER 1

1. The idea of forgetting our source and suffering from delusion is also Platonic; Jewish mysticism first flowered, in the second through eighth centuries, in an environment permeated with

Neoplatonism. Nevertheless, mystical interpretations are generally consonant with rabbinic tendencies, even when they apparently have borrowed some concepts from the surrounding culture.

2. Abraham Joshua Heschel, *Moral Grandeur and Spiritual Audacity: Essays,* ed. Susannah Heschel (New York: Farrar, Straus & Giroux, 1996), p. 6.

3. Rabbi Schneur Zalman of Liadi, founder of Chabad-Lubavitch, explains in *Likutei Amarim: Tanya* (Brooklyn, N.Y.: Kehot Publication Society, 1981; hereafter cited as *Tanya*), 1:23, p. 95, that when a person fulfills God's will by doing one of the *mitzvot* (commandments), the physical action is " ... like a body in relation to the soul, the 'soul' being the Supreme Will [of God] to which it is completely surrendered. In this way, the organs of the human body which perform the commandment ... become a vehicle for the Supreme Will; as, for example, the hand that distributes charity to the poor."

4. Most people are aware that the Torah and rabbinic tradition prescribe many commandments for Jews (the traditional number is 613), but the ancient sages also stated that there are seven Noahide commandments for non-Jews. They derived these from biblical stories during the time of Noah. These commandments embody basic rules of human ethical and spiritual life that had been revealed to all humanity. These include avoiding idolatry, blasphemy, murder, theft, adultery, and injury to animals and setting up courts of justice to administer the laws.

CHAPTER 2

1. Rabbi Nachman of Breslov, "The Turkey Prince," in *Rabbi Nachman's Stories,* trans. Rabbi Aryeh Kaplan (Jerusalem: Breslov Research Institute, 1983), pp. 479–80.

2. Symeon the New Theologian, from *The Moral Speeches*, No. 10, trans. from the Greek Fathers by Elpenor, at www.ellopos.net/elpenor/greek-texts/fathers/symeon-withusgod.asp, retrieved March 2, 2006.

3. Thomas à Kempis, *Imitation of Christ,* Book 2, trans. William Benham (Project Gutenberg, 1999), 4:2.
4. Aryeh Kaplan, *Sefer Yetzirah: The Book of Creation* (York Beach, Maine: Samuel Weiser, 1997), 1:5, p. 44.
5. *Sefer Yetzirah* 1:1, p. 5. Dionysius the Areopagite, *On the Divine Names and the Mystical Theology,* ed. Clarence Edwin Rolt (Grand Rapids, Mich.: Christian Classics Ethereal Library, 2005; originally London: SPCK, 1920), retrievable online at www.ccel.org/ccel/rolt/dionysius.html, accessed March 6, 2006. An important ninth-century Irish-Scottish thinker who revived Christian theology, Johannes Scotus Erigena, also accorded great significance to the names.
6. In addition to the ten *sefirot,* the received tradition of Kabbalah speaks of four "Worlds," from the first emanation of the divine light down to the physical world in which we live. Briefly, they are called Emanation (from God), Creation, Formation, and Action. Each of those worlds corresponds to a letter of God's holy four-letter name. Each world has levels within it; each world, and each level within the worlds, is a veil that masks divinity. Thus, there are more complex dimensions than I can treat in this book.

CHAPTER 3

1. Rabbi Abraham Isaac Kook, *The Lights of Penitence, The Moral Principles, Lights of Holiness, Essays, Letters and Poems,* trans. Ben Zion Bokser (New York: Paulist Press, 1978), p. 225.
2. David Bohm, "Postmodern Science and a Postmodern World," in *The Reenchantment of Science: Postmodern Proposals,* ed. David Ray Griffin (Albany, N.Y.: State University of New York Press, 1988), p. 63.
3. Brian Swimme and Thomas Berry, *The Universe Story: From the Primordial Flaring Forth to the Ecozoic Era: A Celebration of the Unfolding of the Cosmos* (San Francisco: HarperSanFrancisco, 1994), p. 138.

4. *Tanya* 1:37, pp. 166–67. The author is commenting on the verse, "To you it was shown, so that you might know that the Lord is God; there is nothing else beside Him" (Deut. 4:35).

5. *Tanya* 1:2, p. 7; cf. 2:8–9, p. 325.

6. Kaplan, *Sefer Yetzirah,* p. 12. Some interpreters place souls in the next higher level of *sefirot* (*Binah*-Understanding, which corresponds to the world of *Beriah* or Creation).

7. Kook, *Lights of Penitence,* p. 222.

8. Rabbi Nachman of Breslov, *Likutei Moharan* (Jerusalem: Breslov Research Institute, 1986–2000), Lesson 38.

9. Emmanuel Schochet, "Mystical Concepts in Chassidism," in appendix to *Tanya,* p. 846. For a discussion of different philosophies of Kabbalah, see Rabbi Yitzchak Ginsburgh, "Basics in Kabbalah and Chassidut: Three Stages in the Evolution of Kabbalistic Thought," at www.inner.org/stages/stages.htm (Shechem, Israel: 2000), retrieved May 25, 2006.

10. Kaplan, *Sefer Yetzirah,* p. 14.

11. See Samson Raphael Hirsch, commentary on the Pentateuch, Exodus 25.

12. Rabbi Mordecai Miller, *Sabbath Shiurim* [lectures] (Gateshead, England: Gateshead Foundation for Torah, 1969), p. 89.

13. Rabbi Chaim Kramer with Avraham Sutton, *Anatomy of the Soul* (New York: Breslov Research Institute, 1998), pp. 180, 185.

14. See Aryeh Kaplan, *Innerspace: Introduction to Kabbalah, Meditation, and Prophecy* (New York: Moznaim Publishers, 1990), p. 198, n. 19.

CHAPTER 4

1. Swimme and Berry, *Universe Story,* pp. 35, 36.

2. For elaboration, see *Tanya* 2:5, 297–99.

3. Rashi on Genesis 1:1. The commentary of Rashi (Rabbi Shlomo Yitzchak, eleventh century), Judaism's basic biblical commentator, is available in most Hebrew Bibles, and several editions now have English translations or paraphrases of his most important comments.

4. *The Bahir: Illumination,* translation and commentary by Aryeh Kaplan (York Beach, Maine: Samuel Weiser, 1979), Saying no. 135, p. 50.

5. Moshe Chaim Luzzato, *The Knowing Heart,* trans. Shraga Silverstein (New York: Feldheim, 1982), p. 81.

6. Abraham Joshua Heschel, "The Meaning of This Hour," in *Between God and Man,* ed. Fritz A. Rothschild (New York: Free Press, 1997; orig. 1959), pp. 255–57.

7. The Apter Rebbe, *Ohev Yisroel,* Vayetze 15b, quoted in Aryeh Kaplan, *The Light Beyond: Adventures in Hasidic Thought* (New York: Maznaim Publishing, 1981), p. 50.

8. David Ray Griffin, "Of Minds and Molecules: Postmodern Medicine in a Psychosomatic Universe," in *Reenchantment of Science,* ed. Griffin, p. 143.

9. Nachman of Breslov, *Rabbi Nachman's Stories,* pp. 385–89.

CHAPTER 5

1. In Judaism, the rabbinic tradition says that since the destruction of the Temple, three things substitute for sacrifice: prayer, giving to charity, and our table (holiness in eating). These are ways of beginning to "obliterate all ego."

2. See Barbara Ehrenreich, *Blood Rites: The Origins of the Passions of War* (New York: Henry Holt and Company, 1997).

3. This interpretation is based on the biblical verse that designates the seven lower *sefirot:* "Yours, O God, are the Greatness, the Strength, the Beauty, the Victory, and the Glory, for All in heaven and in earth; Yours, O God, is the Kingdom" (1 Chron. 29:11). See Kaplan, *Sefer Yetzirah,* p. 25.

Yesod-Foundation may also include what is popularly called the karmic history of an individual—the term *karma* from Indian philosophies meaning the results of actions that have been performed in all lifetimes. Many kabbalists have also held that souls usually incarnate many times and carry the residue of previous lives into each succeeding one; but you may not incarnate again immediately after completing the round of your previous life—a soul might reincarnate soon, or not again for centuries. It is not necessary, however, to hold a belief in reincarnation to use insights from Kabbalah.

4. While many people have the impression that Judaism's path is described in the Hebrew Bible, this is actually not the case. Judaism's unique construction is called the *mesorah*—usually translated as "tradition." This involves an interpretive community of scholars—the rabbis—who base their decisions on study of the situations and decisions made over some thirty centuries in the framework of the commandments set forth in the written Torah (the first five books of the Hebrew Bible). The set of rules called *halacha* has been established for each generation and each individual by the process of scholars responding to questions that arise in the community and seeking answers in the Torah, according to carefully defined procedures and precedents. This is a powerful system that has helped keep the Jewish community alive and vibrant for thousands of years.

5. Kaplan, *Sefer Yetzirah,* commentary to 1:1.

6. Rupert Sheldrake, *The Presence of the Past: Morphic Resonance and the Habits of Nature* (Rochester, Vt.: Inner Traditions, 1995).

7. Many interpreters of Torah state that change is impermissible and that it has not occurred in authentic Judaism. However, it is widely recognized that different applications have been made. For example, the written Torah explicitly permitted a certain form of slavery, while modifying its negative effects by placing strong restrictions on the master. Eventually, rabbinic tradition forbade slavery. Another example is that capital punishment was prescribed for some infringements of law, but the rabbis created conditions that made it very difficult to apply, so that a Sanhedrin (Supreme Court) that ordered one execution in seventy years was considered a cruel court.

8. Kaplan, *Sefer Yetzirah,* p. 55.

9. *Tanya* 1:4, pp. 15–17.

10. *Tanya* 4:5, p. 415; 4:9, p. 437; emphasis added.
11. For a recent discussion, see Wayne Muller, *Sabbath: Restoring the Sacred Rhythm of Rest* (New York: Bantam Doubleday, 1999).

CHAPTER 6

1. Rabbi Yitzchak Ginsburgh, *The Alef-Beit: Jewish Thought Revealed Through the Hebrew Letters* (Northvale, N.J.: Jason Aronson, 1995), p. 8.
2. See above, chapter 5, note 3. Until around 400 CE the idea of reincarnation was permitted in the early church.
3. *Pirke Avot (Sayings of the Fathers)* 1:4, 3:2. Texts describe *Netzach* and *Hod* as alluding to "Torah scholars," meaning those who devote themselves full time to absorbing and transmitting spiritual teachings.
4. This metaphor is from Connie Kaplan; see *The Woman's Book of Dreams: Dreaming as a Spiritual Practice* (Portland, Ore.: Beyond Words, 1999).
5. The classic expression is in the Torah itself, when the Israelites at Mount Sinai said, *"Na'aseh venishmah,"* "We will do and we will hear." In other words, we will perform the commandments first, and then we will integrate them into our being. As Rabbi Chaim Kramer explains, "The basic premise of the commandments is that once we 'act' in compliance with the objective morality of the Torah, this morality will become part of the spiritual and emotional makeup of the human personality. Thus, the Torah does not directly command us to 'be' but to 'do.'... Its commands are clearly designed by God to impact on our basic character traits, but through our actions" (Kramer, *Anatomy of the Soul,* p. 41).

CHAPTER 7

1. Rashi, commentary on Gen. 2:5.
2. Heschel, "On Prayer," in *Moral Grandeur,* p. 260.

3. Some excellent discussions of these issues can be found in Larry Dossey, *Healing Words: The Power of Prayer and the Practice of Medicine* (San Francisco: HarperSanFrancisco, 1993).

4. "Motivating oneself to settle one's mind enables one to connect one's *Da'at* to *Keter*, i.e. to the spiritual" (Kramer, *Anatomy of the Soul*, p. 193).

5. Reb Noson of Nemirov, *Likutei Halachot, Birkhat HaReiach*, 4:14–16, quoted in Kramer, *Anatomy of the Soul*, p. 163. Similar comments come from the non-Hasidic teacher Rabbi Eliyahu Dessler, who writes that internalizing knowledge, or "returning the knowledge to one's heart," is achieved by use of the imagination. See *Strive for Truth!*, Part 3 (Jerusalem: Feldheim, 1989), p. 235.

6. Samson Raphael Hirsch, *Horeb: A Philosophy of Jewish Laws and Observances* (London: Soncino, 1962), pp. 427–28.

7. See Aryeh Kaplan, *Meditation and the Bible* (York Beach, Maine: Samuel Weiser, 1988).

8. An excellent discussion appears in Rabbi Dessler's "Being and Having," in *Strive for Truth!* part 3, pp. 195–205.

9. For a discussion of the "soul contract," see Connie Kaplan, *The Invisible Garment: 30 Spiritual Principles That Weave the Fabric of Human Life* (San Diego: Jodere Group, 2004).

10. Heschel, "To Be a Jew," *Moral Grandeur*, p. 7.

CHAPTER 8

1. Bohm, "Postmodern Science," p. 67.

2. John Muir, "Mountain Thoughts," in *John of the Mountains,* ed. Linnie Marsh Wolfe (Madison, Wis.: University of Wisconsin Press, 1981 [orig. 1938]), at www.yosemite.ca.us/john_muir_writings/mountain_thoughts.html, retrieved March 6, 2006.

3. See Melvin Morse and Paul Perry, *Parting Visions* (New York: Ballantine Books, 1993).

4. Martin Luther King Jr., *Strength to Love* (Philadelphia: Fortress Press, 1986), p. 124.

5. Aryeh Kaplan, *Meditation and Kabbalah* (York Beach, Maine: Samuel Weiser, 1982), p. 143.

6. The prophet Ezekiel's famous vision of the chariot (Ezek. 1) contains this profound concept. In a verse (which, interestingly, was left out of the Greek translation on which many Christian Bibles are based), the text says simply: "And the living creatures ran and returned like rays of light." This phrase "ran and returned" suggested to the kabbalists that even the angels, who are described as beings that "never swerved in their course" nor deviated from their mission, did not remain in a fixed relationship to God. They were running and returning, as if they were flashing in and out of existence.

7. Kook, *Lights of Penitence,* p. 236.

8. Dessler, *Strive for Truth!* part 3, p. 235.

9. *Meister Eckhart: A Modern Translation*, trans. Robert B. Blakney (New York: Harper & Row, 1941), p. 6.

10. Kook, *Lights of Penitence,* p. 213.

GLOSSARY

Notes on pronunciation: *ch* is pronounced like a guttural *h*, as in Hanukkah.

Modern Israeli Hebrew (as well as the diction of Sephardic Jews) often, but not always, puts a light accent on the last syllable, whereas Ashkenazic Jews may accent the next-to-last syllable, a diction influenced by Yiddish. Thus, *Binah* might be pronounced bee-NAH by an Israeli, but BEE-nah by a rabbi with an Eastern European background. Other differences exist as well. The pronunciations below are generally in accord with Israeli pronunciation.

Adonai (ah-doh-NIGH): A name of God encountered frequently in the Hebrew Bible and used as address to God in the Jewish prayer book; specifically, the pronunciation substituted for the four-letter name of God (Tetragrammaton, often spelled Y-H-V-H in modern texts); usually translated "Lord."

Asiyah (ah-see-YAH): "Action." The fourth and lowest of the Four Worlds according to Kabbalah, namely, the world of action and material form.

Atzilut (ah-tzee-LOOT): "Emanation." The first and highest of the Four Worlds according to Kabbalah, in which God began creating the world by emanating divine energy.

Bahir (bah–HEER): "Brilliance." A well-known mystical text, probably from the eleventh century but possibly much earlier, which describes the structure of the system of *sefirot* almost as they are known today.

Beriah (buh–ree–AH): "Creation." The second of the Four Worlds according to Kabbalah, where God's energy began to take the form of thought.

Binah (bee–NAH): "Understanding." The *sefirah* of the left temple, representing the divine template or matrix of thought forms; nourishes and develops flashes of inspiration from *Chochmah*.

Chesed (CHEH–sehd): "Lovingkindness." The *sefirah* of the right arm, with the quality of expansiveness and outgoing love.

Chochmah (choch–MAH): "Wisdom." The *sefirah* of the right temple, with the quality of surprising creativity, like a lightning-bolt flash of inspiration.

Da'at (dah–AHT): "Knowledge." The *sefirah* located at the brain stem, with the quality of internalizing and unifying knowledge, connecting mind with the lower *sefirot*.

devekut (duh–vay–KOOT): "Clinging." A state of mystical elevation in which the practitioner achieves a profound closeness to God.

Ein Sof (AIN SOAF): "There Is No End." A common kabbalistic term for the Infinite, that is, God, in his most transcendent aspect.

Elohim (el–oh–HEEM): A name of God encountered frequently in the Hebrew Bible, understood in Jewish tradition as divinity active in the laws of the natural world and in purveying justice. *Elohenu* (el–oh–HAY–noo) is the first-person plural possessive, meaning "our God"; this form appears frequently in Jewish prayers as part of address to God.

Gevurah (guh-voo-RAH): "Strength." The *sefirah* of the left arm, with the qualities of restraint, discipline, and withdrawal.

halacha (hah-lah-CHAH): "The walking." The general term for Jewish law.

Hasidism: A popular Jewish religious movement that began in late-eighteenth-century Eastern Europe, fully within the Orthodox framework, emphasizing devotion in prayer, love of one's fellow, and strong relationships between teacher and disciple. Hasidic teachers were noted for their ability to transmit difficult concepts of mysticism to the ordinary person.

Hod (HOAD): "Glory." The *sefirah* of the left hip and leg, understood here as "Surrender," emphasizing the quality of sensing and processing emotional information.

Kabbalah (kah-bah-LAH): "Received." Generally, the Jewish mystical tradition from about the second century CE to the present.

Malkhut (mal-CHOOT): "Kingship." The tenth of the *sefirot*, at the feet, expressing the world as it is normally perceived; also regarded as the final manifestation of divine will.

midah (mee-DAH) (plural, *midot*, mee-DOAT): "Measure." A quality or attribute of a person or of God. In mystical contexts, the word usually refers to one of the six middle *sefirot (Chesed, Gevurah, Tiferet, Netzach, Hod, Yesod)*.

midrash (mee-DRAHSH): The general term for the collections of homiletic and inspirational interpretations of scripture, particularly using stories and word associations, produced during the third to eighth centuries CE.

mitzvah (meetz-VAH) (plural, *mitzvot,* meetz-VOAT): "Commandment."

Netzach (nay-TZAHCH): "Victory." The *sefirah* of the right hip and leg, expressing perseverance and motion.

Sefer Yetzirah (SAY-fair yuh-TZEE-rah): "Book of Creation." An ancient and influential Jewish mystical text, possibly written in an early form in the second century CE, remarkable for its intricate numerological and alphabetical correlations.

sefirot (suh-fee-ROAT) (singular *sefirah,* suh-fee-RAH): The ten divine energies manifested in every process of creation.

Shabbat (shah-BAHT): The seventh day of the week, a holy day of abstaining from work and celebration of rest, observed from before sunset on Friday night to at least an hour after sunset Saturday night.

Shema (sh-MAH): "Hear." The first word of the basic Jewish affirmation of faith, emphasizing the oneness of God ("Hear, O Israel! The Lord is our God, the Lord is One!"); and, by extension, the name of the recitation, twice daily in prayer, of this verse and associated biblical passages.

Talmud (TAL-mood): The records of extensive discussions of Jewish sages on topics of Jewish law and practice, from the third to the sixth centuries, which form the textual core of Judaism from that time onward. While Talmuds were collected and edited in both the Babylonian and the Israelite (Jerusalem) communities, the word *Talmud* usually refers to the more complete Babylonian Talmud unless otherwise noted.

Tanya (TAHN-yah): "It has been taught ... " The first word and common title of the *Sefer Shel Benonim,* or "Book for the Average Person," written by Rabbi Schneur Zalman of Liadi at the turn of the nineteenth century. Originally written for his disciples in the Chabad-Lubavitch group, it is now regarded as a classic of Hasidic philosophy and a great work on spiritual self-improvement.

Tiferet (tee-FAIR-et): "Splendor." The *sefirah* of the heart, expressing the divine-human union of vision and purpose.

Torah (toh-RAH): "Teaching." The first five books of the Hebrew Bible; also, the tradition of teaching and commentary based on those books and on the rest of the Bible.

tzimtzum (tzeem-TZOOM): "Contraction." The withdrawal of divine energy into itself at the beginning of creation, allowing a space to be "vacated" in which a universe could emerge. Metaphorically, the word can mean personal withdrawal of energy.

Yesod (yuh-SOAD): "Foundation." The *sefirah* of the pelvic region, with the quality of channeling and transmitting sexual, karmic, and social energy.

Yetzirah (yuh-tzee-RAH): "Formation." The third of the Four Worlds according to Kabbalah, denoting the stage of creation in which things are given their distinct energetic qualities.

Zohar (ZOH-har): "Radiance." A classic mystical text whose sources are claimed to go back to a famous second-century rabbi, Shimon bar Yochai. It was published and widely circulated beginning in the thirteenth century and provides the foundation for most modern Jewish mystical schools of thought.

SUGGESTIONS FOR FURTHER READING

Dan, Joseph. *Kabbalah: A Very Short Introduction.* New York: Oxford University Press, 2006.

Frankiel, Tamar. *The Gift of Kabbalah: Discovering the Secrets of Heaven, Renewing Your Life on Earth.* Woodstock, Vt.: Jewish Lights Publishing, 2001.

Frankiel, Tamar, and Judy Greenfeld. *Entering the Temple of Dreams: Jewish Prayers, Movements, and Meditations for the End of the Day.* Woodstock, Vt.: Jewish Lights Publishing, 2000.

——. *Minding the Temple of the Soul: Balancing Body, Mind, and Spirit Through Traditional Jewish Prayer, Movement, and Meditation.* Woodstock, Vt.: Jewish Lights Publishing, 1997.

Green, Arthur. *Ehyeh: A Kabbalah for Tomorrow.* Woodstock, Vt.: Jewish Lights Publishing, 2004.

——. *Seek My Face: A Jewish Mystical Theology.* Woodstock, Vt.: Jewish Lights Publishing, 2003.

Kramer, Chaim, ed. and trans. *Anatomy of the Soul.* Jerusalem: Breslov Research Institute, 1998.

Kushner, Lawrence. *The Way Into Jewish Mystical Tradition.* Woodstock, Vt.: Jewish Lights Publishing, 2001.

Nachman of Breslov. *The Lost Princess & Other Kabbalistic Tales of Rebbe Nachman of Breslov.* Translated by Aryeh Kaplan. Woodstock, Vt.: Jewish Lights Publishing, 2005.

————. *The Seven Beggars & Other Kabbalistic Tales of Rebbe Nachman of Beslov.* Translated by Aryeh Kaplan. Woodstock, Vt.: Jewish Lights Publishing, 2005.

Spirituality/Lawrence Kushner

The Book of Letters: A Mystical Hebrew Alphabet
Popular HC Edition, 6 x 9, 80 pp, 2-color text, 978-1-879045-00-2 **$24.95**
Collector's Limited Edition, 9 x 12, 80 pp, gold foil embossed pages, w/limited edition silkscreened print, 978-1-879045-04-0 **$349.00**

The Book of Words: Talking Spiritual Life, Living Spiritual Talk
6 x 9, 160 pp, Quality PB, 978-1-58023-020-9 **$16.95**

Eyes Remade for Wonder: A Lawrence Kushner Reader   *Introduction by Thomas Moore*
6 x 9, 240 pp, Quality PB, 978-1-58023-042-1 **$18.95**

God Was in This Place & I, i Did Not Know: Finding Self, Spirituality and Ultimate Meaning   6 x 9, 192 pp, Quality PB, 978-1-879045-33-0 **$16.95**

Honey from the Rock: An Introduction to Jewish Mysticism
6 x 9, 176 pp, Quality PB, 978-1-58023-073-5 **$16.95**

Invisible Lines of Connection: Sacred Stories of the Ordinary
5½ x 8½, 160 pp, Quality PB, 978-1-879045-98-9 **$15.95**

Jewish Spirituality—A Brief Introduction for Christians
5½ x 8½, 112 pp, Quality PB, 978-1-58023-150-3 **$12.95**

The River of Light: Jewish Mystical Awareness
6 x 9, 192 pp, Quality PB, 978-1-58023-096-4 **$16.95**

The Way Into Jewish Mystical Tradition
6 x 9, 224 pp, Quality PB, 978-1-58023-200-5 **$18.99**; HC, 978-1-58023-029-2 **$21.95**

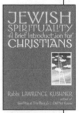

Bible Study/Midrash

Abraham's Bind & Other Bible Tales of Trickery, Folly, Mercy and Love   *By Michael J. Caduto*
Re-imagines many biblical characters, retelling their stories and highlighting their foibles and strengths, their struggles and joys. Readers will learn that God has a way of working for them and through them, even today.
6 x 9, 224 pp, HC, 978-1-59473-186-0 **$19.99** *(A SkyLight Paths book)*

Ancient Secrets: Using the Stories of the Bible to Improve Our Everyday Lives
By Rabbi Levi Meier, PhD 5½ x 8½, 288 pp, Quality PB, 978-1-58023-064-3 **$16.95**

The Genesis of Leadership: What the Bible Teaches Us about Vision, Values and Leading Change   *By Rabbi Nathan Laufer; Foreword by Senator Joseph I. Lieberman*
Unlike other books on leadership, this one is rooted in the stories of the Bible, and teaches the values that the Bible believes are prerequisites for true leadership.
6 x 9, 288 pp, HC, 978-1-58023-241-8 **$24.99**

Hineini in Our Lives: Learning How to Respond to Others through 14 Biblical Texts and Personal Stories   *By Norman J. Cohen* 6 x 9, 240 pp, Quality PB, 978-1-58023-274-6 **$16.99**

Moses and the Journey to Leadership: Timeless Lessons of Effective Management from the Bible and Today's Leaders   *By Dr. Norman J. Cohen* 6 x 9, 250 pp, HC, 978-1-58023-227-2 **$21.99**

Self, Struggle & Change: Family Conflict Stories in Genesis and Their Healing Insights for Our Lives   *By Norman J. Cohen* 6 x 9, 224 pp, Quality PB, 978-1-879045-66-8 **$18.99**

The Triumph of Eve & Other Subversive Bible Tales   *By Matt Biers-Ariel*
5½ x 8½, 192 pp, HC, 978-1-59473-040-5 **$19.99** *(A SkyLight Paths book)*

Voices from Genesis: Guiding Us through the Stages of Life   *By Norman J. Cohen*
6 x 9, 192 pp, Quality PB, 978-1-58023-118-3 **$16.95**

Or phone, fax, mail or e-mail to: **JEWISH LIGHTS** Publishing
Sunset Farm Offices, Route 4 • P.O. Box 237 • Woodstock, Vermont 05091
Tel: (802) 457-4000 • Fax: (802) 457-4004 • www.jewishlights.com
Credit card orders: **(800) 962-4544** (8:30AM–5:30PM ET Monday–Friday)
Generous discounts on quantity orders. SATISFACTION GUARANTEED. Prices subject to change.

Children's Books
by Sandy Eisenberg Sasso

Adam & Eve's First Sunset: God's New Day
Engaging new story explores fear and hope, faith and gratitude in ways that will delight kids and adults—inspiring us to bless each of God's days and nights.
9 x 12, 32 pp, Full-color illus., HC, 978-1-58023-177-0 **$17.95** *For ages 4 & up*

Also Available as a Board Book: **Adam and Eve's New Day**
5 x 5, 24 pp, Full-color illus., Board, 978-1-59473-205-8 **$7.99** *For ages 0–4 (A SkyLight Paths book)*

But God Remembered
Stories of Women from Creation to the Promised Land
Four different stories of women—Lillith, Serach, Bityah, and the Daughters of Z—teach us important values through their faith and actions.
9 x 12, 32 pp, Full-color illus., HC, 978-1-879045-43-9 **$16.95** *For ages 8 & up*

Cain & Abel: Finding the Fruits of Peace
Shows children that we have the power to deal with anger in positive ways. Provides questions for kids and adults to explore together.
9 x 12, 32 pp, Full-color illus., HC, 978-1-58023-123-7 **$16.95** *For ages 5 & up*

God in Between
If you wanted to find God, where would you look? This magical, mythical tale teaches that God can be found where we are: within all of us and the relationships between us.
9 x 12, 32 pp, Full-color illus., HC, 978-1-879045-86-6 **$16.95** *For ages 4 & up*

God's Paintbrush: Special 10th Anniversary Edition
Wonderfully interactive, invites children of all faiths and backgrounds to encounter God through moments in their own lives. Provides questions adult and child can explore together.
11 x 8½, 32 pp, Full-color illus., HC, 978-1-58023-195-4 **$17.95** *For ages 4 & up*

Also Available: **God's Paintbrush Teacher's Guide**
8½ x 11, 32 pp, PB, 978-1-879045-57-6 **$8.95**

God's Paintbrush Celebration Kit
A Spiritual Activity Kit for Teachers and Students of All Faiths, All Backgrounds
Additional activity sheets available:
8-Student Activity Sheet Pack (40 sheets/5 sessions), 978-1-58023-058-2 **$19.95**
Single-Student Activity Sheet Pack (5 sessions), 978-1-58023-059-9 **$3.95**

In God's Name
Like an ancient myth in its poetic text and vibrant illustrations, this award-winning modern fable about the search for God's name celebrates the diversity and, at the same time, the unity of all people.
9 x 12, 32 pp, Full-color illus., HC, 978-1-879045-26-2 **$16.99** *For ages 4 & up*

Also Available as a Board Book: **What Is God's Name?**
5 x 5, 24 pp, Board, Full-color illus., 978-1-893361-10-2 **$7.99** *For ages 0–4 (A SkyLight Paths book)*

Also Available: **In God's Name video and study guide**
Computer animation, original music, and children's voices. 18 min. **$29.99**

Also Available in Spanish: **El nombre de Dios**
9 x 12, 32 pp, Full-color illus., HC, 978-1-893361-63-8 **$16.95** *(A SkyLight Paths book)*

Noah's Wife: The Story of Naamah
When God tells Noah to bring the animals of the world onto the ark, God also calls on Naamah, Noah's wife, to save each plant on Earth. Based on an ancient text.
9 x 12, 32 pp, Full-color illus., HC, 978-1-58023-134-3 **$16.95** *For ages 4 & up*

Also Available as a Board Book: **Naamah, Noah's Wife**
5 x 5, 24 pp, Full-color illus., Board, 978-1-893361-56-0 **$7.95** *For ages 0–4 (A SkyLight Paths book)*

For Heaven's Sake: Finding God in Unexpected Places
9 x 12, 32 pp, Full-color illus., HC, 978-1-58023-054-4 **$16.95** *For ages 4 & up*

God Said Amen: Finding the Answers to Our Prayers
9 x 12, 32 pp, Full-color illus., HC, 978-1-58023-080-3 **$16.95** *For ages 4 & up*

Meditation

The Handbook of Jewish Meditation Practices
A Guide for Enriching the Sabbath and Other Days of Your Life
By Rabbi David A. Cooper Easy-to-learn meditation techniques.
6 x 9, 208 pp, Quality PB, 978-1-58023-102-2 **$16.95**

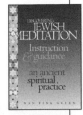

Discovering Jewish Meditation: Instruction & Guidance for Learning an Ancient
Spiritual Practice *By Nan Fink Gefen*
6 x 9, 208 pp, Quality PB, 978-1-58023-067-4 **$16.95**

A Heart of Stillness: A Complete Guide to Learning the Art of Meditation
By David A. Cooper 5½ x 8½, 272 pp, Quality PB, 978-1-893361-03-4 **$16.95** *(A SkyLight Paths book)*

Meditation from the Heart of Judaism: Today's Teachers Share Their
Practices, Techniques, and Faith *Edited by Avram Davis*
6 x 9, 256 pp, Quality PB, 978-1-58023-049-0 **$16.95**

Silence, Simplicity & Solitude: A Complete Guide to Spiritual Retreat at Home
By David A. Cooper 5½ x 8½, 336 pp, Quality PB, 978-1-893361-04-1 **$16.95**
(A SkyLight Paths book)

The Way of Flame: A Guide to the Forgotten Mystical Tradition of Jewish
Meditation *By Avram Davis* 4½ x 8, 176 pp, Quality PB, 978-1-58023-060-5 **$15.95**

Ritual/Sacred Practice/Journaling

The Jewish Dream Book: The Key to Opening the Inner Meaning of
Your Dreams *By Vanessa L. Ochs with Elizabeth Ochs; Full-color illus. by Kristina Swarner*
Instructions for how modern people can perform ancient Jewish dream practices
and dream interpretations drawn from the Jewish wisdom tradition.
8 x 8, 128 pp, Full-color illus., Deluxe PB w/flaps, 978-1-58023-132-9 **$16.95**

The Jewish Journaling Book: How to Use Jewish Tradition to Write
Your Life & Explore Your Soul *By Janet Ruth Falon*
Details the history of Jewish journaling throughout biblical and modern times, and
teaches specific journaling techniques to help you create and maintain a vital journal,
from a Jewish perspective. 8 x 8, 304 pp, Deluxe PB w/flaps, 978-1-58023-203-6 **$18.99**

The Book of Jewish Sacred Practices: CLAL's Guide to Everyday & Holiday
Rituals & Blessings *Edited by Rabbi Irwin Kula and Vanessa L. Ochs, PhD*
6 x 9, 368 pp, Quality PB, 978-1-58023-152-7 **$18.95**

Jewish Ritual: A Brief Introduction for Christians
By Rabbi Kerry M. Olitzky and Rabbi Daniel Judson
5½ x 8½, 144 pp, Quality PB, 978-1-58023-210-4 **$14.99**

The Rituals & Practices of a Jewish Life: A Handbook for Personal Spiritual
Renewal *Edited by Rabbi Kerry M. Olitzky and Rabbi Daniel Judson*
6 x 9, 272 pp, illus., Quality PB, 978-1-58023-169-5 **$18.95**

The Sacred Art of Lovingkindness: Preparing to Practice
By Rabbi Rami Shapiro 5½ x 8½, 176 pp, Quality PB, 978-1-59473-151-8 **$16.99**
(A SkyLight Paths book)

Science Fiction/Mystery & Detective Fiction

Mystery Midrash: An Anthology of Jewish Mystery & Detective Fiction
Edited by Lawrence W. Raphael; Preface by Joel Siegel
6 x 9, 304 pp, Quality PB, 978-1-58023-055-1 **$16.95**

Criminal Kabbalah: An Intriguing Anthology of Jewish Mystery & Detective Fiction
Edited by Lawrence W. Raphael; Foreword by Laurie R. King
6 x 9, 256 pp, Quality PB, 978-1-58023-109-1 **$16.95**

Wandering Stars: An Anthology of Jewish Fantasy & Science Fiction
Edited by Jack Dann; Introduction by Isaac Asimov
6 x 9, 272 pp, Quality PB, 978-1-58023-005-6 **$16.95**

More Wandering Stars: An Anthology of Outstanding Stories of Jewish Fantasy and
Science Fiction *Edited by Jack Dann; Introduction by Isaac Asimov*
6 x 9, 192 pp, Quality PB, 978-1-58023-063-6 **$16.95**

Theology/Philosophy

Christians and Jews in Dialogue: Learning in the Presence of the Other
By Mary C. Boys and Sara S. Lee; Foreword by Dr. Dorothy Bass
A guide for members of any faith tradition who want to move beyond the rhetoric of interfaith dialogue and into the demanding yet richly rewarding work of developing new understandings of the religious other—and of one's own tradition.
6 x 9, 240 pp, HC, 978-1-59473-144-0 **$21.99** *(A SkyLight Paths Book)*

The Death of Death: Resurrection and Immortality in Jewish Thought
By Neil Gillman 6 x 9, 336 pp, Quality PB, 978-1-58023-081-0 **$18.95**

Ethics of the Sages: *Pirke Avot*—Annotated & Explained
Translation & Annotation by Rabbi Rami Shapiro
5½ x 8½, 208 pp, Quality PB, 978-1-59473-207-2 **$16.99** *(A SkyLight Paths Book)*

Evolving Halakhah: A Progressive Approach to Traditional Jewish Law
By Rabbi Dr. Moshe Zemer 6 x 9, 480 pp, Quality PB, 978-1-58023-127-5 **$29.95**;
HC, 978-1-58023-002-5 **$40.00**

Hasidic Tales: Annotated & Explained
By Rabbi Rami Shapiro; Foreword by Andrew Harvey
5½ x 8½, 240 pp, Quality PB, 978-1-893361-86-7 **$16.95** *(A SkyLight Paths Book)*

Healing the Jewish-Christian Rift: Growing Beyond our Wounded History
By Ron Miller and Laura Bernstein; Foreword by Dr. Beatrice Bruteau
6 x 9, 288 pp, Quality PB, 978-1-59473-139-6 **$18.99** *(A SkyLight Paths book)*

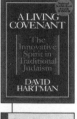

A Heart of Many Rooms: Celebrating the Many Voices within Judaism
By David Hartman 6 x 9, 352 pp, Quality PB, 978-1-58023-156-5 **$19.95**

The Hebrew Prophets: Selections Annotated & Explained
Translation & Annotation by Rabbi Rami Shapiro; Foreword by Zalman M. Schachter-Shalomi
5½ x 8½, 224 pp, Quality PB, 978-1-59473-037-5 **$16.99** *(A SkyLight Paths book)*

A Jewish Understanding of the New Testament
By Rabbi Samuel Sandmel; Preface by Rabbi David Sandmel
5½ x 8½, 368 pp, Quality PB, 978-1-59473-048-1 **$19.99** *(A SkyLight Paths book)*

Keeping Faith with the Psalms: Deepen Your Relationship with God Using the Book of Psalms *By Daniel F. Polish* 6 x 9, 320 pp, Quality PB, 978-1-58023-300-2 **$18.99**;
HC, 978-1-58023-179-4 **$24.95**

A Living Covenant: The Innovative Spirit in Traditional Judaism
By David Hartman 6 x 9, 368 pp, Quality PB, 978-1-58023-011-7 **$20.00**

Love and Terror in the God Encounter
The Theological Legacy of Rabbi Joseph B. Soloveitchik
By David Hartman 6 x 9, 240 pp, Quality PB, 978-1-58023-176-3 **$19.95**;
HC, 978-1-58023-112-1 **$25.00**

The Personhood of God: Biblical Theology, Human Faith and the Divine Image
By Dr. Yochanan Muffs; Foreword by Dr. David Hartman
6 x 9, 240 pp, HC, 978-1-58023-265-4 **$24.99**

Tormented Master: *The Life and Spiritual Quest of Rabbi Nahman of Bratslav*
By Arthur Green 6 x 9, 416 pp, Quality PB, 978-1-879045-11-8 **$19.99**

Traces of God: Seeing God in Torah, History and Everyday Life
By Neil Gillman 6 x 9, 240 pp, HC, 978-1-58023-249-4 **$21.99**

We Jews and Jesus: Exploring Theological Differences for Mutual Understanding
By Rabbi Samuel Sandmel; Preface by Rabbi David Sandmel
6 x 9, 176 pp, Quality PB, 978-1-59473-208-9 **$16.99** *(A SkyLight Paths book)*

Your Word Is Fire: The Hasidic Masters on Contemplative Prayer
Edited and translated by Arthur Green and Barry W. Holtz
6 x 9, 160 pp, Quality PB, 978-1-879045-25-5 **$15.95**

Theology/Philosophy/The Way Into... Series

The Way Into... series offers an accessible and highly usable "guided tour" of the Jewish faith, people, history and beliefs—in total, an introduction to Judaism that will enable you to understand and interact with the sacred texts of the Jewish tradition. Each volume is written by a leading contemporary scholar and teacher, and explores one key aspect of Judaism. *The Way Into...* series enables all readers to achieve a real sense of Jewish cultural literacy through guided study.

The Way Into Encountering God in Judaism
By Neil Gillman
For everyone who wants to understand how Jews have encountered God throughout history and today.
6 x 9, 240 pp, Quality PB, 978-1-58023-199-2 **$18.99**; HC, 978-1-58023-025-4 **$21.95**
Also Available: **The Jewish Approach to God:** A Brief Introduction for Christians
By Neil Gillman
5½ x 8½, 192 pp, Quality PB, 978-1-58023-190-9 **$16.95**

The Way Into Jewish Mystical Tradition
By Lawrence Kushner
Allows readers to interact directly with the sacred mystical text of the Jewish tradition. An accessible introduction to the concepts of Jewish mysticism, their religious and spiritual significance and how they relate to life today.
6 x 9, 224 pp, Quality PB, 978-1-58023-200-5 **$18.99**; HC, 978-1-58023-029-2 **$21.95**

The Way Into Jewish Prayer
By Lawrence A. Hoffman
Opens the door to 3,000 years of Jewish prayer, making available all anyone needs to feel at home in the Jewish way of communicating with God.
6 x 9, 224 pp, Quality PB, 978-1-58023-201-2 **$18.99**

The Way Into Judaism and the Environment
By Jeremy Benstein
Explores the ways in which Judaism contributes to contemporary social-environmental issues, the extent to which Judaism is part of the problem and how it can be part of the solution.
6 x 9, 288 pp, HC, 978-1-58023-268-5 **$24.99**

The Way Into Tikkun Olam (Repairing the World)
By Elliot N. Dorff
An accessible introduction to the Jewish concept of the individual's responsibility to care for others and repair the world.
6 x 9, 320 pp, HC, 978-1-58023-269-2 **$24.99**

The Way Into Torah
By Norman J. Cohen
Helps guide in the exploration of the origins and development of Torah, explains why it should be studied and how to do it.
6 x 9, 176 pp, Quality PB, 978-1-58023-198-5 **$16.99**; HC, 978-1-58023-028-5 **$21.95**

The Way Into the Varieties of Jewishness
By Sylvia Barack Fishman
Explores the religious and historical understanding of what it has meant to be Jewish from ancient times to the present controversy over "Who is a Jew?"
6 x 9, 250 pp, HC, 978-1-58023-030-8 **$24.99**

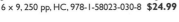

Spirituality

The Adventures of Rabbi Harvey: A Graphic Novel of Jewish Wisdom and Wit in the Wild West *By Steve Sheinkin*
Jewish and American folktales combine in this witty and original graphic novel collection. Creatively retold and set on the western frontier of the 1870s.
6 x 9, 144 pp, Full-color illus., Quality PB, 978-1-58023-310-1 **$16.99**

Ethics of the Sages: Pirke Avot—Annotated & Explained
Translation and Annotation by Rabbi Rami Shapiro
5½ x 8½, 192 pp, Quality PB, 978-1-59473-207-2 **$16.99** *(A SkyLight Paths book)*

A Book of Life: Embracing Judaism as a Spiritual Practice
By Michael Strassfeld 6 x 9, 528 pp, Quality PB, 978-1-58023-247-0 **$19.99**

Meaning and Mitzvah: Daily Practices for Reclaiming Judaism through Prayer, God, Torah, Hebrew, Mitzvot and Peoplehood *By Rabbi Goldie Milgram*
7 x 9, 336 pp, Quality PB, 978-1-58023-256-2 **$19.99**

The Soul of the Story: Meetings with Remarkable People
By Rabbi David Zeller 6 x 9, 288 pp, HC, 978-1-58023-272-2 **$21.99**

Aleph-Bet Yoga: Embodying the Hebrew Letters for Physical and Spiritual Well-Being
By Steven A. Rapp. Foreword by Tamar Frankiel, PhD and Judy Greenfeld. Preface by Hart Lazer.
7 x 10, 128 pp, b/w photos, Quality PB, Layflat binding, 978-1-58023-162-6 **$16.95**

Entering the Temple of Dreams
Jewish Prayers, Movements, and Meditations for the End of the Day
By Tamar Frankiel, PhD, and Judy Greenfeld
7 x 10, 192 pp, illus., Quality PB, 978-1-58023-079-7 **$16.95**

Does the Soul Survive? A Jewish Journey to Belief in Afterlife, Past Lives & Living with Purpose *By Rabbi Elie Kaplan Spitz; Foreword by Brian L. Weiss, MD*
6 x 9, 288 pp, Quality PB, 978-1-58023-165-7 **$16.99**

First Steps to a New Jewish Spirit: Reb Zalman's Guide to Recapturing the Intimacy & Ecstasy in Your Relationship with God *By Rabbi Zalman M. Schachter-Shalomi with Donald Gropman* 6 x 9, 144 pp, Quality PB, 978-1-58023-182-4 **$16.95**

God in Our Relationships: Spirituality between People from the Teachings of Martin Buber *By Rabbi Dennis S. Ross* 5½ x 8½, 160 pp, Quality PB, 978-1-58023-147-3 **$16.95**

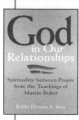

Judaism, Physics and God: Searching for Sacred Metaphors in a Post-Einstein World
By Rabbi David W. Nelson 6 x 9, 368 pp, Quality PB, inc. reader's discussion guide, 978-1-58023-306-4 **$18.99**;
HC, 352 pp, 978-1-58023-252-4 **$24.99**

The Jewish Lights Spirituality Handbook: A Guide to Understanding, Exploring & Living a Spiritual Life *Edited by Stuart M. Matlins*
What exactly is "Jewish" about spirituality? How do I make it a part of my life?
Fifty of today's foremost spiritual leaders share their ideas and experience with us.
6 x 9, 456 pp, Quality PB, 978-1-58023-093-3 **$19.99**

Bringing the Psalms to Life: How to Understand and Use the Book of Psalms
By Daniel F. Polish 6 x 9, 208 pp, Quality PB, 978-1-58023-157-2 **$16.95**;
HC, 978-1-58023-077-3 **$21.95**

God & the Big Bang: Discovering Harmony between Science & Spirituality
By Daniel C. Matt 6 x 9, 216 pp, Quality PB, 978-1-879045-89-7 **$16.99**

Minding the Temple of the Soul: Balancing Body, Mind, and Spirit through Traditional Jewish Prayer, Movement, and Meditation *By Tamar Frankiel, PhD, and Judy Greenfeld*
7 x 10, 184 pp, illus., Quality PB, 978-1-879045-64-4 **$16.95**
Audiotape of the Blessings and Meditations: 60 min. **$9.95**
Videotape of the Movements and Meditations: 46 min. **$20.00**

One God Clapping: The Spiritual Path of a Zen Rabbi *By Alan Lew with Sherril Jaffe*
5½ x 8½, 336 pp, Quality PB, 978-1-58023-115-2 **$16.95**

There Is No Messiah ... and You're It: The Stunning Transformation of Judaism's Most Provocative Idea *By Rabbi Robert N. Levine, DD*
6 x 9, 192 pp, Quality PB, 978-1-58023-255-5 **$16.99**

These Are the Words: A Vocabulary of Jewish Spiritual Life
By Arthur Green 6 x 9, 304 pp, Quality PB, 978-1-58023-107-7 **$18.95**

Inspiration

God's To-Do List: 103 Ways to Live Your Purpose for Doing God's Work on Earth
By Dr. Ron Wolfson 6 x 9, 150 pp, Quality PB, 978-1-58023-301-9 **$15.99**

God in All Moments: Mystical & Practical Spiritual Wisdom from Hasidic Masters
Edited and translated by Or N. Rose with Ebn D. Leader
5½ x 8½, 192 pp, Quality PB, 978-1-58023-186-2 **$16.95**

Our Dance with God: Finding Prayer, Perspective and Meaning in the Stories of Our
Lives *By Karyn D. Kedar* 6 x 9, 176 pp, Quality PB, 978-1-58023-202-9 **$16.99**

Also Available: **The Dance of the Dolphin** (HC edition of *Our Dance with God*)
6 x 9, 176 pp, HC, 978-1-58023-154-1 **$19.95**

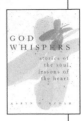

The Empty Chair: Finding Hope and Joy—Timeless Wisdom from a Hasidic Master,
Rebbe Nachman of Breslov *Adapted by Moshe Mykoff and the Breslov Research Institute*
4 x 6, 128 pp, 2-color text, Deluxe PB w/flaps, 978-1-879045-67-5 **$9.95**

The Gentle Weapon: Prayers for Everyday and Not-So-Everyday Moments—
Timeless Wisdom from the Teachings of the Hasidic Master, Rebbe Nachman of Breslov
Adapted by Moshe Mykoff and S. C. Mizrahi, together with the Breslov Research Institute
4 x 6, 144 pp, 2-color text, Deluxe PB w/flaps, 978-1-58023-022-3 **$9.99**

God Whispers: Stories of the Soul, Lessons of the Heart *By Karyn D. Kedar*
6 x 9, 176 pp, Quality PB, 978-1-58023-088-9 **$15.95**

An Orphan in History: One Man's Triumphant Search for His Jewish Roots
By Paul Cowan; Afterword by Rachel Cowan. 6 x 9, 288 pp, Quality PB, 978-1-58023-135-0 **$16.95**

Restful Reflections: Nighttime Inspiration to Calm the Soul, Based on Jewish Wisdom
By Rabbi Kerry M. Olitzky & Rabbi Lori Forman 4½ x 6¼, 448 pp, Quality PB, 978-1-58023-091-9 **$15.95**

Sacred Intentions: Daily Inspiration to Strengthen the Spirit, Based on Jewish Wisdom
By Rabbi Kerry M. Olitzky and Rabbi Lori Forman 4½ x 6¼, 448 pp, Quality PB, 978-1-58023-061-2 **$15.95**

Kabbalah/Mysticism/Enneagram

Awakening to Kabbalah: The Guiding Light of Spiritual Fulfillment
By Rav Michael Laitman, PhD 6 x 9, 192 pp, HC, 978-1-58023-264-7 **$21.99**

Seek My Face: A Jewish Mystical Theology *By Arthur Green*
6 x 9, 304 pp, Quality PB, 978-1-58023-130-5 **$19.95**

Zohar: Annotated & Explained
Translation and annotation by Daniel C. Matt; Foreword by Andrew Harvey
5½ x 8½, 176 pp, Quality PB, 978-1-893361-51-5 **$15.99** *(A SkyLight Paths book)*

Cast in God's Image: Discover Your Personality Type Using the Enneagram and Kabbalah
By Rabbi Howard A. Addison
7 x 9, 176 pp, Quality PB, Layflat binding, 20+ journaling exercises, 978-1-58023-124-4 **$16.95**

Ehyeh: A Kabbalah for Tomorrow
By Arthur Green 6 x 9, 224 pp, Quality PB, 978-1-58023-213-5 **$16.99**

The Enneagram and Kabbalah, 2nd Edition: Reading Your Soul
By Rabbi Howard A. Addison 6 x 9, 192 pp, Quality PB, 978-1-58023-229-6 **$16.99**

Finding Joy: A Practical Spiritual Guide to Happiness *By Dannel I. Schwartz with Mark Hass*
6 x 9, 192 pp, Quality PB, 978-1-58023-009-4 **$14.95**

The Flame of the Heart: Prayers of a Chasidic Mystic *By Reb Noson of Breslov. Translated by
David Sears with the Breslov Research Institute* 5 x 7¼, 160 pp, Quality PB, 978-1-58023-246-3 **$15.99**

The Gift of Kabbalah: Discovering the Secrets of Heaven, Renewing Your Life on Earth
By Tamar Frankiel, PhD 6 x 9, 256 pp, Quality PB, 978-1-58023-141-1 **$16.95;**
HC, 978-1-58023-108-4 **$21.95**

Kabbalah: A Brief Introduction for Christians
By Tamar Frankiel, PhD 5½ x 8½, 208 pp, Quality PB, 978-1-58023-303-3 **$16.99**

The Lost Princess and Other Kabbalistic Tales of Rebbe Nachman of Breslov
The Seven Beggars and Other Kabbalistic Tales of Rebbe Nachman of Breslov
Translated by Rabbi Aryeh Kaplan; Preface by Rabbi Chaim Kramer
Lost Princess: 6 x 9, 400 pp, Quality PB, 978-1-58023-217-3 **$18.99**
Seven Beggars: 6 x 9, 192 pp, Quality PB, 978-1-58023-250-0 **$16.99**

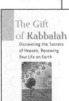

See also *The Way Into Jewish Mystical Tradition* in Spirituality / The Way Into... Series

About Jewish Lights

People of all faiths and backgrounds yearn for books that attract, engage, educate, and spiritually inspire.

Our principal goal is to stimulate thought and help all people learn about who the Jewish People are, where they come from, and what the future can be made to hold. While people of our diverse Jewish heritage are the primary audience, our books speak to people in the Christian world as well and will broaden their understanding of Judaism and the roots of their own faith.

We bring to you authors who are at the forefront of spiritual thought and experience. While each has something different to say, they all say it in a voice that you can hear.

Our books are designed to welcome you and then to engage, stimulate, and inspire. We judge our success not only by whether or not our books are beautiful and commercially successful, but by whether or not they make a difference in your life.

For your information and convenience, at the back of this book we have provided a list of other Jewish Lights books you might find interesting and useful. They cover all the categories of your life:

Bar/Bat Mitzvah	Life Cycle
Bible Study / Midrash	Meditation
Children's Books	Parenting
Congregation Resources	Prayer
Current Events / History	Ritual / Sacred Practice
Ecology	Spirituality
Fiction: Mystery, Science Fiction	Theology / Philosophy
Grief / Healing	Travel
Holidays / Holy Days	12-Step
Inspiration	Women's Interest
Kabbalah / Mysticism / Enneagram	

Stuart M. Matlins, Publisher

Or phone, fax, mail or e-mail to: **JEWISH LIGHTS Publishing**
Sunset Farm Offices, Route 4 • P.O. Box 237 • Woodstock, Vermont 05091
Tel: (802) 457-4000 • Fax: (802) 457-4004 • www.jewishlights.com
Credit card orders: **(800) 962-4544** (8:30AM–5:30PM ET Monday–Friday)
Generous discounts on quantity orders. SATISFACTION GUARANTEED. Prices subject to change.

For more information about each book, visit our website at www.jewishlights.com